Terence Michael Shannon

The Enlightenment Series

Get Over Your Drama Already

Rewire your Mind, Body and Soul
to Live a Happy Life

Black Rose Writing | Texas

©2020 by Terence Michael Shannon
All rights reserved. No part of this book may be reproduced, stored in a retrieval system or transmitted in any form or by any means without the prior written permission of the publishers, except by a reviewer who may quote brief passages in a review to be printed in a newspaper, magazine or journal.

The author grants the final approval for this literary material.

First printing

This is a work of fiction. Names, characters, businesses, places, events, and incidents are either the products of the author's imagination or used in a fictitious manner. Any resemblance to actual persons, living or dead, or actual events is purely coincidental.

ISBN: 978-1-68433-510-7
PUBLISHED BY BLACK ROSE WRITING
www.blackrosewriting.com

Printed in the United States of America
Suggested Retail Price (SRP) $18.95

Get Over Your Drama Already is printed in Sabon

*As a planet-friendly publisher, Black Rose Writing does its best to eliminate unnecessary waste to reduce paper usage and energy costs, while never compromising the reading experience. As a result, the final word count vs. page count may not meet common expectations.

Dedicated to my son, mom, dad, brothers, aunts, uncles, sister-in-law, nephews, niece, cousins, friends, and all their families. Life is a journey; thank you for believing and putting up with me.

"I believe people can change with an idea. The idea we are all here for a purpose and to live a happy life filled with love for all."
Terence Michael Shannon

When reading, reflect on your life and correlate the stories to yours and grow from these experiences. Life is designed as an inner journey of love, knowledge, and forgiveness, explore that in your mind. The book was written during a personal journey of my life. It was an enlightening period as I continued my quest to seek a higher knowledge in the spiritual realm of the mind, body, and soul. I am not a doctor, just a simple man writing a book to help others. The stories and suggestions guide you to explore your mind and jump-start you to recognize your journey to happiness should you choose. I do not take any responsibility or liability for any actions/reactions caused in your life. Be open and apply wisely.

Contents

Terms	
Introduction	
Life	
The Journey's Beginning	
The Journey Starter	1
Ego	9
Vibration	16
Karma	20
The Foundation of Life	25
The Universe	29
Connecting to the Universe	38
Conscious vs. Subconscious Mind	43
How your Brain is Wired	47
The Little Voice Inside	52
Letting Go	55
Everything has a Season	62
The Path	68
The Energy	74
Fear	81
Love	85
Finding Yourself	89
Loving Yourself	95
Pay Attention	102
Living in the Present	108
Bubble to Bubble	111
The Mirror	117
The Little Box	122
Broken Heart Syndrome	128
Changing the Lives of Others	134
Be Yourself	140
Social Media	144
Friendship	146
Parenting	149
Learning to Say No	154
Rest	158
Deadly Sins of Life	161
Exercise your Mind, Body and Soul	164
The Phoenix	167
The Journey Continues	173
Side Notes	
About the Author	
Note from the Author	

Terms

The Journey – Phrase used to describe a person's natural progression as they grow in the understanding of a higher power, the universe, earth, and themselves. At the heart of the journey is the knowledge it is a journey for the enlightenment of one's self-love, one's life purpose, ending the toxic ego, letting go of the past and learning the karmic lessons of this lifetime.

Vibrational Frequency – An energy source within us, an electricity, a vibration that operates in our heart and soul. The inner connection to all living things. It's determined, raised, or lowered by the thoughts about ourselves and others. It emits an aura or attraction from one's soul to attract the lessons, people, dreams, and purpose of this lifetime.

3D-State of Consciousness – You are human and live in a world of subconscious and awareness of things, material possessions, "what I own." The focus of all thought is on the external world of what people think of me, "what I can do, how pretty I am," power, greed, the chasing of flesh, and you allow this to be your value—the ego of the flesh and materialistic things.

4D-State of Consciousness – You are still human, live in the 3D world, and integrate the consciousness that you are a spirit that flesh surrounds.

You start to question your spirituality, what you stand for, and where your life is headed. You understand the sacred nature of people, life, souls, existence, karma, the lesson of this lifetime, and empathy. You know your soul is your value.

Ego (Egoic Thoughts) – A collection of beliefs and past experiences that defines how a person interacts with life. An unconscious inside voice tells us we are smarter, superior, in control, judgmental, and right all the time. It tells us no one loves us and is self-destroying. The seeking of constant acceptance from others, self-beauty, and material possessions is what one places as their value.

Karma – The sum of a person's actions in this and previous lives deciding their fate in future existences. In the western world, how you treat people, hurt them, or steal from them will happen to you in return so that you can experience the pain. The hard lessons of life are to heal oneself of all their karma.

Soul – The spiritual or immaterial part of a human being or animal, regarded as immortal.

Living in the Present – Paying attention to the present moment, time is an illusion, and your mind is pulled into the past or the future, or both. Surrender to what is right now and commit to being there, completely. Life will take care of the rest.

The Foundation – Underlying basis or principle for something. Every aspect of life, especially relationships of all kinds, requires substance, mainly enjoyment, love, and trust. There must be a foundation for any structure or relationship to be built and stand the test of time.

The Path – Life's twists and turns. The hardships and joys of learning what and who we are and why we are even alive. A divine plan laid out for us that we must recognize to understand our purpose in life by learning the karmic lessons of this lifetime. The understanding to decipher the messages you receive from within.

Living by the Spirit – A connection to something bigger than ourselves, a search for meaning in life, and a sense of purpose. When one learns to live by their intuition instead of their thoughts of the flesh, one releases their ego and acts on what their heart tells them. Their desires and their mind no longer lead one; their spirit guides them.

The Source – The creation, explosion, power, and infinite wisdom of the universe.

Dark Night of the Soul – Reaching the lowest point in this incarnation. A contract you made with your soul before you were born on this earth that involved everyone who led you to this point. A blessing in disguise and a spiritual cleansing gives you an understanding of why everything happened the way it did for you to find meaning in life.

The Little Box – The overall attraction by all when the beauty of the female species is present. The understanding the most beautiful creature the universe created is feminine, it's beauty, that's all and is the way it has always been since the beginning of time. Every being notices a beautiful female; the male species takes it a step further.

The Churn – The constant speed of life, societal pressures, emphasis on money, lack of respect and values, constantly checking smartphones, the removal of the higher power from everything, the little box, the downfall of the family, the stress all this causes in life and how people react to it.

INTRODUCTION

"It is easy to change yourself for a while, then fall prey to the same old lifestyle. The hard part is to change your thoughts from the flesh to the spirit. Desires of the flesh are the egos and evil of the world; love is the fruit of the spirit."
– Terence Shannon

Do you ever wonder where your life is headed? Who you are? Why you think the way you do? What is your purpose? Life is beautiful and a journey of learning who we are and why we are even alive on a rock floating around in space. At the end of a lifetime, one usually realizes it was a quest for what we have done and what we wished we would have changed. It is then too late to realize you can't take your money, cars, spouse, significant other, children, anything tangible with you except your soul. Wouldn't it be nice to understand what makes our lives happy along the journey without regrets?

Most people do not realize the divine plan laid out for them and live in a world of drama filled with fear, guilt, shame, desires of the flesh, and wealth. They choose to take the daily bait thrown out by others, the information on television, the internet, their past, and the minute struggles of everyday life. They allow these thoughts to drive their entire life. When you step back from those thoughts and recognize we are all here for a reason, you understand the soul's lessons. The lessons of life itself. Everything we feel, say, do, or think is recorded. We go through life accumulating a balance sheet, debits, and credits. All our actions, thoughts, and emotions that are out of alignment with the universe's dogma of love will need to be repaid with forgiveness and compassion. Every thought, every action, no matter how small, needs to be paid back with love. That is our karma.

Karma surrounds us and is way bigger than most of us are aware. It affects your life in every way. When you perform any action, karma creates a memory, which creates desire and leads to another action. Every situation and everyone you meet has a karmic significance, and everything happens for a reason. Eventually, karma gets everyone, and you will experience an event in life that will open the flood gates to suffering. Whether that is a near-death experience, a serious illness, a diagnosis of cancer, the loss of a loved one, a huge setback, a childhood tragedy, or a romantic breakup. These are all lessons of life and lessons of the soul to guide you back to your path. By looking inward, forgiving yourself, forgiving others, and loving yourself, you can release the pain and find your happiness.

Your ego plays a huge role in comprehending this journey. This understanding will only develop by eradicating your egocentric voice and following the spirit inside you. The tests are childhood tragedies, loss of loved ones, betrayals, and setbacks. Every situation in life is a test of your ego. The lessons of these tests will lead one, should one understand, to the journey within to release the negative emotions driving their thoughts.

And to spread the light of love to all living creatures. The lessons learned by extinguishing our egoic thoughts is the cleansing of our soul and a path to your meaning. By practicing positive internal thoughts with the understanding that love for yourself is the journey, we allow ourselves to let go of our ego. That action then becomes the building block or the foundation of finding balance in one's life, one's soul.

The lessons of love, forgiveness, compassion, and empathy are the only paybacks when you venture through the journey within. It's how you grow spiritually from these experiences that allow us to understand our life lessons. Once we have understood our inner journey, we are led by our soul to realize we are spirits having a human experience, and we can accomplish anything we believe in our hearts and minds. When we believe, we understand that we are all on a journey to live by love, love for all, and, most importantly, love for thyself.

Comprehending this inner journey is to understand how we choose to live our life. When we learn empathy for others and ourselves, we have an awareness to change our lives and others' lives with our actions and thoughts. We grow spiritually. We can forgive and channel our energy towards our life and to learn about ourselves. We learn that one's wasted energy directed away from one's life's lessons and filled with the world's drama blocks one's joy. We learn to pay attention to our relationships with others and understand our relationship with ourselves. We open to the awareness that our thoughts are the magnet to the external world, and what one thinks about themselves is what they attract in return. We accept all internal emotions have been self-induced and brought about by the self. We understand all pain is self-induced through thought. It's that understanding that allows us to change our thoughts and overcome the pain, heal, and connect to our soul.

Our soul teaches us by guiding us to the people and experiences to teach us our life lessons. When one can understand that inner voice and follow it, the light of love begins to enter the soul. It guides us to accept the hurtful events we allow to hold us back. It allows us to move on from the past, forgive, and begin living a joyful life. It brings about a new outlook on life in which one feels blessed to be alive. One begins to see the beauty of the world, the beauty of all living things, and one has empathy for all. One heals themselves of all the accumulated suffering and finds inner joy in all facets of life. By allowing yourself to recognize and learn the lessons, one can choose to move away from the internal pain and external distractions to the love for self. One then becomes free, and life's blessings are endless.

Paying attention to one's life and one's loved one's life is what life is all about, love, people, and the love of people. By using self-love, self-forgiveness, the forgiveness of others, and the connection to the universe, one will be filled with the knowledge and attract one's life ambitions. The answers are there, search within, and listen to that inner voice as all the consciousness is inside you. The open gates of abundance from the universe await you to figure out the private lessons and shower your life with love and joy. Ponder that when you are reading through the book.

Namaste

LIFE

"Just as a candle cannot burn without fire, humankind cannot live without a spiritual life."
– Buddha

What is life? Do you think about that anymore, the miracle of being alive? Most do not. Many of us live in an endless loop within ourselves; the past and not the present. Sometimes, when we experience some form of a letdown, our parents, our spouse, a mistake, or some teacher, we get stuck at that moment. We allow ourselves to become a victim or believe as they believe. We choose to do this. We fall back to that moment when something negative happens to us. Many of us do not understand that every hardship, letdown, and setback is a lesson somewhere filled with abundance and love. When we learn to let go of the negative and forgive people and ourselves, we release the emotion holding us back. Nothing must hurt in life unless we allow and choose to let it. Quit wasting today thinking about yesterday. I do not know a better way to say that. Letting go of all the bad things in our past allows our present and future to be much brighter. The real journey begins when we learn to let go of our history and live with love.

Where is all the love in the world? Is love inside you? Life is a mystery, just like love. Understanding and unlocking the mystery of life within ourselves is the journey. The journey lasts until we pass away into the universe. Along the way, when a part of the journey ends, there is always a new beginning. My journey began long ago when I was five years old; however, through many books, relationships, and life's twists and turns, it started again. I was in a funk and started thinking about my life. After much reflection, reality crept in; I was going through the motions in my life and mind.

One day I woke up not knowing what to do with my life. I started to introspect on a deep level. What was I going to do with my existence? I had no idea; however, I knew I had to do something. An image surfaced through meditation one day to become hypersensitive to my surroundings and pay attention to every thought, lesson, and people. I decided to let go of the past, do the right thing as much as possible, and changed how I thought about life, myself, and others.

After much thought and absorbing the world around me, I began writing to help myself through the first world problems I was facing. I had not written much, only my senior thesis to graduate from college and a few love letters. However, through countless interactions, I realized that a large segment of men and women in society experienced many of the same issues. They had no clue what their life was about or where they were going. Many were lost to the meaning, clung to the past, and wondered why they were so unhappy. I decided to continue writing using research and personal stories to help others with the hope of opening their minds to address their past. I wrote this book intending to change others' lives with my thoughts and experiences to gain the wisdom and understanding that we are all on a journey. My goal is to help start your inner journey to find joy, self-love, and meaning in life. We all need help in some facet of our existence.

We live in dangerous times in a misguided world full of many troubles, desires, religions, politics, divisive movements, diseases, smartphones, the internet, power struggles, greed, and many external influences. Many people are jealous of others and want to destroy them. Everything has turned into a political battle. People are taking sides. Here you are in this part of your life, taking the time to read a self-help book. Good for you! Welcome to a new beginning; should you choose your new life. The journey can be somewhat painful; let's start by being honest with each other.

I have always thought about everything in my life and let them fade until I was in my late thirties and early forties. I'm a Virgo, you know, the astrological sign that must think everything through, tough sometimes. Through many relationships and distancing myself from perceived friends, I did not recognize and understand that I lacked love for myself. I say this because of my thoughts and my actions not only towards others; however, by the way, I treated myself when something did not go my way. I then started to reflect on myself for answers. At the time, I was a lost man who thought the world was a certain way and meandered through life, not paying attention to my relationship with myself, life and the universe. I was too afraid to dive in for fear that I would look upon myself as a failure. However, through the process, I realized my relationships with others, the world, and myself were misguided. Not only I and many others did not understand the essential things in life, like family, friendship, unconditional love, self-love, altruism, and the things you cannot touch like faith, hope, and trust. I did not realize that the reality you see through your eyes and feel through your heart is not always the reality you create in your mind. I recognized your eyes could deceive you, and the truth of someone's thoughts may be way different on the inside. I began to live in the actual reality of life, in the present moment, not what was in my head and began to see the clarity of consciousness. I began to live by the spirit and acted the way it told me.

I then realized that the older I got, the less I knew. I realized the struggle was within, not with the external world. I realized all pain is self-induced, no matter how anyone had treated me. I understood you choose to be whatever you want in life; a hero or a victim. I finally understood all relationships I participated in were leading me somewhere, no matter how they began or ended. I realized that only you control your emotions and happiness. That many people lived through their egotistical thoughts, greed, and the flesh. They forgot about love and lived their lives; however, they wanted with or without the consequences. That realization led me to let go of negative experiences and mental attachments. I climbed out of the proverbial box I placed myself in, dove into my issues, and explored things to the core. I began to use love in all interactions, which I had not done as a kid or an adult.

Growing up, I was fearful of just about everything in life. I traveled through my life being fearful, mainly of the future, my past mistakes, my health, my job, and what people thought about me, I think you get it. So, I told my confused, crazy mind, that's it, change, change, or you will never find happiness. That is when the enlightenment moment began. What did I do?

I understood our thoughts direct our movie and create the attractions in life to our happiness. I realized thought was one of the six basic senses, not the overall feeling. I then began following my spirit and acting as it instructed me. I consciously attempted to do the right thing all the time and speak in a respectful way. I anchored love in my motives. I removed people from my life that did not respect themselves or me. I began friendships for the right reasons. I began to be comfortable in my skin and spread kindness. I increased my level of helping others. I spent my precious time with the people who loved and cared about me. I started thinking of others instead of myself. I realized the hardships and pain I had encountered were leading me to learn lessons. I learned that the relationships I was attracting were the precise ones to show a hidden meaning to serve my evolution. I understood life is precious and not about me; it was about me learning to love myself and others and to spread that love.

I then dove into myself and shed light on all the darkness that held me back. I had figured out that my brother's death in nineteen-eighty-nine was not a place where I should park my life. I had connected to my soul and started to pay attention to what it was guiding me to. Life changed all around me. I received a promotion at work, people started asking me over for gatherings, people seemed to be more beautiful; I think that was reality. People I knew and strangers started seeking me for advice; in the end, I became happier, and so did the people around me. I had let go of all the perceived behaviors we learn as adults that tell us how we are "supposed" to be. I understood when we set up the wrong expectations for attending any event or participating in any relationship was a setup for failure. I began to be myself and be confident with who I was. I realized we do not control anything except our thoughts and emotions. I turned over control to the universe. I learned that should you want to make the universe laugh, tell it how your plans should play out. Those actions instilled the wisdom that the journey of life is to find unconditional love for yourself.

Finding love for yourself is the journey. When we incorporate loving ourselves, believe in our self, and connect to our soul and the universe, the world around us changes. That action brings clarity to our life's dreams. Events will develop and attract what all those inner thoughts have been telling us our entire life. We will understand our life's meaning; however, the lessons will cloud that path along the way. Those hard lessons lead to wounds that need healing and create trapped, past emotions we allow to control our everyday life. We heal those wounds by helping others using the knowledge gained from our painful experiences and by shining the light of love through the cracks on all that darkness. We use forgiveness of ourselves and others.

We all make mistakes; we must learn the lesson. When you move into the 4D world of thinking, we use our conscious mind to live in the present, away from the past's negative energy. We live by the spirit and follow the voice inside of us. By letting go of the past, we release the emotional energy drowning out the voice inside us. We become free on the inside and feel the weight lifted. That action guides us on the path to understanding our life, to let go of our egoic thoughts, to use love to solve everything, and to connect to our soul. It leads to an understanding that a loving relationship with our self and others is the foundation of life.

Eventually, through this process, you will no longer allow the drama of the day, people, television, words, or actions to control your happiness. You will learn just to change the tire on any adverse events and keep moving down the road. That lesson will prepare you for some dark defining moment in life, like losing a job, a loved one, or a relationship breakup. You will have the ability to remove the darkness and replace it with the light of love. You will understand it's a lesson leading you to the love of yourself. You will learn to overcome any obstacle without destroying yourself. Instead of saying, "why me," you say, "try me." You understand the beauty of the world and everything around you. You know the grace of you and the love of yourself. You see, the journey within is the only journey that will ever make you joyful. You stop blaming others and the outside world for everything. You understand that no matter how far or how fast you run, you can never get away from yourself. You learn to take the advice you give others and apply it to yourself. You understand that everything connects for a reason in your life. You need to step back, decipher the message, and learn from it. You realize that life is about healing the soul, love of self, people, and people's love.

Your value and purpose are already inside you. Take the quiet alone time to recognize how valuable you already are and do not allow people or possessions to determine that. Understand that you are loved unconditionally from the universe; that's why you are here in the first place, be happy, spread love, and figure out what's already inside your mind and soul. To figure out your life lessons, manifest your thoughts into reality, develop loving relationships, and find meaning in life.

Through the book, we will be discussing many adaptations using loving actions to solve internal and external issues, relationships, and self-thoughts. We will explore ways to transform your thinking process to rewire your mind, body, and soul to display a framework to live a happy, fruitful life that you share with others. I will challenge you to think differently about yourself by reflecting on how you feel about everything by opening your mind to think outside your egoic thoughts (divisive thoughts of others and self.) Realize and recognize your feelings when you feel the world and people should be a certain way and turn out to be different. Keep you from rushing to judgment of yourself, feeling hurt, or anger. Realize the reality you live in and learn to live with clarity to elevate your life, thoughts, and dreams. How to build relationship foundations and explore ways to open your mind to the many possibilities of life and what life has to offer. Let go of people, desires, attachments and possessions. Release the negative thoughts you harbor in your subconscious by forgiving others. Begin the inner journey to discover your meaning in life. Combine the loving thoughts about yourself and others with your mind, body, and soul to form your overall frequency and the aura you exude. This internal vibration is the law of attraction, which is the law of life and the law of the universe. The one dominant force that surrounds and connects us all.

Let's start by discovering how to begin the journey.

The Journey's Beginning

"Every journey has a beginning, middle, and end. It's the memories created by the outpouring of love during the journey that changes the soul forever."
– Terence Shannon

These steps are designed to incorporate into your life, not for the day, throughout every day in combination with each other. Start slow and attempt some of the steps. You do not have to follow them as listed, just when you are comfortable.

Step 1 – Start loving yourself with your thoughts, speech, and the food you consume. Do some research on diets and see where you can replace your food intake from anything with cholesterol and high fat, to fruits and vegetables. Start thinking about what you are grateful for instead of negative thoughts. Get some sleep.

Step 2 – Do a life check every day, meaning, should you have said or done something that bothers you. Ask for forgiveness from the universe, and whomever, you feel this way towards. Forgive yourself and learn the lesson.

Step 3 – Write down everything you feel angry, guilty, or ashamed about. Think about whether you, the action or other people are at fault. Give it some time.

Step 4 – Forgive yourself of everything you wrote down from step 3 and all others involved, no matter what.

Step 5 – Call your parents, siblings, children, whomever you love, and thank them for all they have done for you. Should you have harmful or abusive parents, step-parents, relatives, siblings, or children, write them a letter of how you feel, tell them you love them, and forgive them.

Step 6 – Call, I suggest this the most, write or text everyone you wrote down on your list or feel you hurt in some way. Apologize and ask for their forgiveness. Let the conversation flow from the heart, should they not forgive you, forgive yourself and let it go. Leave a message should they not answer or text that you would like to speak when they have time and want to clear the air.

Step 7 – Should no one respond to your apologies, relax; you did your part and have released some negative energy.

Step 8 – Let go of social pressures, social media posts, politics, religions, race, gender, the news, anything that divides people. Instead, spend time with the ones you love and put the smartphone down. Control your own life, do not allow ideologies or others to drive your emotions. Life is tough; however, life is about love, not anger.

Step 9 – When you go anywhere, find something to be grateful for instead of something you do not like. Take the high road in all situations.

Step 10 – Distance yourself from all dysfunctional friends, lovers, places, anywhere you feel something negative in your chest and stay away from it. This action does not mean your parents or children; you are stuck with them. Instead, understand that every issue in a relationship is an opportunity to fix something.

Step 11 – Take some time and reflect on your progress.

Step 12 – Write down all your dreams and goals in life. Place the list somewhere in your home to see it every day. Read the list and focus your energy daily. Then, anytime you are having dark or lonely thoughts, grab the list and focus your energy on how to accomplish these ideas.

Step 13 – When the people you distanced yourself from, and you are sure there is no avenue to a good relationship attempt to come back into your life, say no thank you to everything. Harsh, I understand; however, you are here to be happy. Letting go is a big step. Take your time.

Step 14 – Wake up every day with a thought of gratitude for being alive and for what you have.

Step 15 – Begin exercising, reading ten pages of a book and meditate even for two minutes, this will help you sleep better.

Step 16 – Realize the process should now be kicking in, and you are not thinking about some of the negative things that bothered you anymore.

Step 17 – Find new places to go. Invite only the people you feel comfortable with, or you know, are looking out for your best interests.

Step 18 – Reflect and repeat whatever steps you feel need any additional work.

Step 19 – Find a new hobby, walking, painting, reading, writing, exercising at home or a gym, anything new to work your mind, body, and soul.

Step 20 – Stay informed, however, end the process of watching the news, smartphone, or social media all day. Limit yourself and use the rest of your time to focus your energy on your loved ones and your life.

Step 21 – When you meet anyone, anywhere, unless there is an emergency of some kind or are communicating with your loved ones, begin staying off your phone. Should someone play with their phone for meaningless reasons, let them know how silly they are for wasting a valuable moment to create memories. Kids need to be taught this; however, adults need to learn this practice also. This alone will help you communicate with people.

Step 22 – Stay positive.

Step 23 – Instead of worrying about your kids, money, yourself, pray instead for a great outcome. Worrying does not help anyone.

Step 24 – Tell your significant other how you feel about them and discuss your future. This action will reduce the anxiety associated with your closest relationship.

Step 25 – Realize the peace inside that may be setting in now.

Step 26 – Search and believe for a new job, whatever positive you like and makes you feel good. Believe in yourself. This step does not include alcohol or drugs.

Step 27 – Leave people alone or stop giving them advice unless they ask. This action does not apply to children, parents, and spouses. There should always be open communication.

Step 28 – Figure out what makes you happy minus the fleshly desires and worldly possessions.

Step 29 – Pay off everything, causing you financial pain. Instead, find something you enjoy that you do not spend money doing. We are programmed to buy things, and that's what supposed to make us happy. Save, not spend. Only ourselves, love, people, and the love of people can make us happy.

Step 30 – Let go of anyone at this stage that brings drama to your life. Should that be close relationships, now is the time to figure out what the issues are. Remember, problems are an opportunity to fix a relationship; however, you will never mend some things from a person's past. Only you can fix you, and only you can change you. A relationship takes two, and both need to want the same outcome for the relationship to be healthy.

Step 31 – Focus your energy on your dreams. When you focus your energy, what you seek will find you.

Step 32 – Say and do the right thing all the time or as much as possible, no matter the situation. Treat everyone with love and kindness, even the people who you perceived hurt or betrayed you. That does not mean to spend time with them.

Step 33 – Meditate and ask the universe for the answers to anything you cannot figure out in life. The answers will appear when you least expect it, be ready.

Step 34 – Should someone close to you pass away or have passed away and affect you daily or your life, reflect and forgive them or yourself for anything that bothers you. Talk to them when you are alone. Remember, someone who loved you, and you loved wants you to move on, let go and live a fruitful life. Should you need to honor them, make sure, their grave has a headstone and is taken care of or start a foundation in their name. The main thing to remember is the universe put them in your life for a reason to teach you something, and they were a blessing no matter how things transpired here on earth.

Step 35 – Be ready to die every day by using love and forgiveness with yourself and others. That way, should you pass on, things will be peaceful, and any remaining negative energy with people you have touched here on earth will have dissipated. You never know when the universe will call you.

Keep all these steps moving forward. The universe forgives us for all our mistakes, give it time to take shape in your life. Good luck and use love and forgiveness along the way.

Get Over Your Drama Already

THE JOURNEY STARTER

"Life is a journey, and it's about growing and changing and coming to terms with who and what you are and loving who and what you are."
– Kelly McGillis

After much reflection, I realized that my cognitive life journey began in San Antonio, Texas, when I was eight or nine years old. Actually, before that, as when I was five, a kindergartener, and almost beat up by a fifth-grader walking home from elementary school. It was like being attacked by a giant. Luckily, my older middle brother showed up and saved me, oh the fear. We'll say that is the beginning of the consciousness of the "real world." I did many fun and beautiful things as a kid; however, I will focus on a few here. I got in trouble a bunch in elementary school, nothing serious. Pondered during house chores, spent a lot of time alone in my backyard playing, was on a four-time city championship swim team, played middle school football, basketball, and track, played high school football/baseball, college baseball, and learned many life lessons. As I grew older, I faced many challenges, mostly playing sports, which molded me into who I became. My journey began again with my brother's death in nineteen-eighty-nine. From there, I was asleep in life, not paying attention, as I will reference in the book. However, the people I encountered in my enlightening period brought to light what was inside me through all those years. Let's explore the journey.

I was surrounded by older people when I was young. I have fifty-three first cousins, two older brothers, and four older boys who lived next door. Except two cousins, I was the youngest of the them. We did all kinds of fun stuff, played many sports, popped fireworks, played board games, rode bikes, played cards, attended countless weddings and family parties; you name it. They were older and moving on in life, college, and whatever else they were interested in, average. That somewhat left me alone to play by myself most times in my backyard. I wasn't sad here or anything as I used to ride BMX bikes all over the neighborhood and town with my buddies, "The Midnight Riders," however spent some quality alone time in my backyard. Funny as I have an older woman friend who is very spiritual who always tells me that she saw me in my backyard playing alone, by the fence away from the house. It was true, so I didn't know what to think; twilight zone stuff.

When I attended elementary school, and we were in gym class or on the playground, suddenly, I had these kids, my age, that I could dominate, most of them as some older brothers. I would pull pranks, tackle them on the playground when we played football, or nail them in the head with the ball when we played kickball, nothing to hurt people, I never thought of hurting people, just having fun. That is how I ran into trouble in my early years. However, along this journey, I always protected younger, smaller kids from bullies and mob mentality kids. So, for me, elementary school was somewhat a double-edge sword of good versus evil. This struggle went on through school, and in fifth grade, I was not allowed to become a patrol; the cross-guard group with stop signs, vests, and badges that escorts kids across intersections. Even though some of the guys in my neighborhood did some of the same things I did at school, they were allowed; I never understood. We all know there are dynamics and a power structure to everything.

One day, I said this is my neighborhood, I do not need to stop for patrols as there were no cars, and I lived three blocks from the school. I did this all the time without patrols. I peddled through the intersection and mocked the patrols, that action had me reported and there I was talking with the gym coach who ran the patrols, Miss Henserling; yes, I have a good memory. She pulled me out of class and tore me a new one that day out by the playground. I never cried or was upset, even though she was, as all I could think about is why I wasn't allowed to be a patrol like all those other guys were who did the same stuff as me. Now I was an A student and everything, honors classes, etc. I began to think about how all this stuff works in the grownup world. I figured out that they were teaching me a lesson. That is how the journey started and changed my behavior, moving forward to middle school and life.

I proceeded to middle school and, at the same time, moved on from my church baseball league, where I had played my entire life to a senior league, thirteen to fifteen-year-old program. The school was terrific; however, I didn't know anyone at the baseball league. I was drafted to the Yankees and became good friends with the coach, his son, and everyone on the team. My training and discipline from elementary school taught me to hold back and not ruffle feathers anymore. I melted in and played an great season as a youngster at second base and pitched some. I earned a position on the thirteen-year-old All-Star team. Everybody on the All-Star team had been playing together since they were five or six. There were the dynamics, the power structure stuff. I played some, however, watched more. In the end, I had a great time and bonded with all these guys. I still communicate with some of them today. Frankly, it was a magical summer of fun.

In the next years of middle school, I played quarterback on the A-Team and baseball in the summer. In the summer of nineteen eighty-six, I joined the fourteen and fifteen-year-old All-Star team, my final year in the league. I played some, and some folks played that should not have. After much fanfare from my mother and other parents who saw the structure costing us, I pitched that final game. That was a teaching moment again in the grownup world. I learned that sometimes people are put into positions by others not by their ability, however by their connections. As the old saying goes, "It's not what you know; it's who you know." What an epiphany for a fifteen-year-old. I began another journey.

I started high school, and there were ups and downs, and things were simple, nothing major that was a huge learning point or made me grow and figure something out except girls. That's another story, and I will leave that to another time. About at the end of my junior year, my brother was killed in an automobile accident. Then suddenly, overnight, there was the journey, which turned out to be an endless journey of searching. I chose to feel sorry for myself. This tragedy caused me to go underground with my thoughts, emotions, character; you name it. I slid through my senior year playing football; I was the punter and caught some balls as a receiver. On the baseball team, I pitched to a ten and two record and earned some city-wide awards. I received a half scholarship to play college baseball at St. Edward's University in Austin, Texas, and moved through the motions. I graduated, got married, and we had a son—standard stuff. After a few years, I got divorced, and that sent me further into this dark journey I had been traveling. However, inside, I always thought about spiritual stuff and would brush it aside.

I moved into an apartment in the summer of nineteen-ninety-seven and hung at this pool for seven years; yes, I had a job. I met a wealth of characters from drug dealers to alcoholics to some guy wanted by the FBI for beating his girlfriend in another state. It was eye-opening on several levels as I didn't realize the structure of the world outside my bubble. I moved out and on from that environment. We come to almost the present, and I move into this resort community, go out and earn a good-paying job, and began to ponder life and my journey.

Then it all came to a head in my mind, the journey was not what I thought it was, it was inside me the whole time, and I felt it. The journey and understanding became clear. I was awake, and I was afraid. I then told myself that I would not be fearful of anything in life anymore. I began to be honest with myself, others, live in the truth, own my actions, and finally understood only you control your happiness. You choose to have fun in life or not. You decide to hang on to the past and use it as an excuse to hold you back. You enable the dark always to overtake the light. When you learn to let go of everything in the past, you change. You understand nothing matters in life except what you will be thinking about on your deathbed. It frees you from life's struggles, and you regain your inner joy, your positive energy. That energy gave me the strength to overcome the hurdle of my brother dying as I shined a light through the emotional wounds on all that darkness. I learned to accept reality, not what I wished happened, or why it happened. I understood what letting go, forgiveness, and love can do and started living a fruitful life. Just like you can.

I then began to study on all levels. After some research, I discovered I had crossed over and passed through the term "The Dark Night of the Soul." Defined as reaching the lowest point of this present life incarnation. It was a poem written by St. John of the Cross while he was in jail for expressing his spirituality. It guides you to let go of meaningless things and to the love of the universe. It states the only light in this dark night is that which burns in the soul. It goes on to state you made a contract with your soul before you were born here on earth that involved everyone who led you to this point. It's a blessing in disguise and a spiritual cleansing that gives you an understanding of why everything happened the way it did to understand your meaning in life. It's the loss of ego, and when we do this, we longer associate ourselves with society's preconception of who we are. It gives us an appreciation for all that is good in life and how little we need to be happy. It connects us with our consciousness and gives us a new outlook on life as you stop blaming other people and look within for answers. You learn forgiveness, love, and gratitude for everything in your life. You realize that you had to go through these tough experiences to get you pointed in a new direction that leads you to become who you are. You begin to trust the universe and turn your life over to that understanding and accept that you are not in control. You make the connection between your mind, body, and soul. You understand that we are much more than our physical body, we are energetic, multidimensional, spiritual beings having a human physical experience, not the other way around. When you think this way and train your mind to, you become aware of who you are and reclaim all your energy. You understand you are not smarter than the universe and follow its laws.

Our minds and our soul are potent tools. When you look within and understand yourself is when you begin the journey. You can never experience joy in your life by hiding and covering everything inside; it stays there. That's what many people do in our world these days; they do not get it out. They never find a way to get the emotions out. They never understand that when you are vulnerable, it is when you learn. They enable the darkness to destroy the joy and happiness of their life.

For me, the realization was, do you think someone you love and who loved you who died wants you to be miserable? Do you think they want you to destroy yourself? The answer is hell no. That epiphany led me to remove the dark thoughts about my past and replace them with the light of loving thoughts. It guided me to learn the past and mistakes were the enemy. I removed all labels from myself. I learned mistakes were like fear and letting go, a path to a new place. As most people will define you by your mistakes, I learned you identify you. You are what you think you are as your spirit is always guiding you. In the end, the universe does not judge you on mistakes; only people do. Let the mistakes and past go, so you will not miss what the world has in store.

That takes me closer to the present. You have started to develop a sense of what my journey was to this point. As you continue, open your mind to the journey of your life. I stated earlier my journey was brought about by many experiences, people, life, death, and relationships. It made me look within my soul and figure out what I stand for, who I am, and what I wanted my future to become. It forced me to understand the journey of life is to find love for ourselves. That we are already whole, we do not need or to seek anything to complete us. We are already complete; we just need to let go of all the things inside that tell us the opposite.

Look back now and remember some of your relationships and ask yourself, what happened? Your parents? That friend? That romantic other? What I am telling you is that you are on a journey. We all are to figure out our meaning in life, pursue it, and find love and happiness along the way. To bring love to ourselves and enjoyment to people.

Do your best to stay away from all the bait and labels people throw at you. Control your journey. Understand that the hurt, betrayal, and lessons guide you to something amazing in your life; it's the path. Those are the deep roots that you must go through to become the abundant fruit tree. The deeper you go within yourself, the higher the abundance. To build the foundation for the growth to occur in your life. Comprehend that all the wounds will heal with forgiveness and listen to your inner voice to be confident. The war within is about good and evil, the dark side, and the force. The struggle of expansion or contraction of the self. One of growth in spirit or to get stuck in the painful relationships and memories of the 3D world.

The journey is inside you already; the love is in your soul. Let the drama go. Live in the present and let go of the past. Then remove the fearful thoughts of the future, instead prepare for it. Prepare yourself for everything by learning the knowledge so you do not fear it or fear presenting the information. That will set you free of being the prisoner, and your journey will become clear. End your journey of life with a smile, not regret and use love to get there. Let's explore ways to understand your journey and set a course for an enlightenment period to propel yourself to experience a happy life.

EGO

"The ego is only an illusion, but a very influential one. Letting the ego illusion become your identity can prevent you from knowing your true self. Ego, the false idea of believing that you are what you have or what you do, is a backward way of assessing and living life."
– Wayne Dyer

Do you ever wonder why close relationships fail? Maybe even your own? Why people seem more interested in their job than their marriage? Ever wonder why people associate success with possessions? Why people seem so lost these days and place importance on how they look or how much money they make? Why people value a material object over people? Ever wonder why so many people are overweight, ill, or on so many pills? Why are so many upset about politics and traffic? That's the ego. What is ego? Ego is a collection of beliefs and past experiences that defines how a person interacts with life. The ego is a good thing when we are confident and do things from our hearts. It gives us the courage and the ability to overcome our fears. However, the wrong side of the ego seems to exist in abundance these days.

Ego is the voice inside that guides us through everything. It pulls us into the past or the future. It keeps us in all the drama of life. It holds us in history to a negative experience, a false belief, something you deem unfair. It blames your parents, makes you a victim, pulls at you, and makes you doubt yourself. It blames your significant other for your unhappiness. It's fear, shame, guilt, and all the negative emotions felt from our experiences. It creates scenarios to keep you stuck in life and not happy. The ego speaks to us all day and guides our interactions. For example, I wonder what that person who is staring at me is thinking? Is my hair messed up, am I ugly, are they attracted to me, do I deserve someone like that? That is the ego's voice we all hear.

The ego is what keeps one in all the drama of life. Many do not even know their ego exists; they just see life the way they see it. They do not understand how they think, interact, judge, love, work, and live may be driven by their ego. They are unconscious to it. Many of the truths we cling to and how we react, depend on our point of view. Life can be cruel and painful and designed to overcome your ego to bring you closer to the unconditional love of the universe. Should you not, your ego will keep you stuck, upset, and always searching in the past. Let's explore the ego, so you understand that everything you thought was real in life may not be, or maybe it's according to your ego.

As children, we have been trained by schools, television, and our parents to be a certain way. That's the tale we have heard repeatedly. What our government and whoever raised us to believe it is. You are married, three kids, a big home, in debt, a good-paying job, two cars, five televisions, smartphones, smart devices, fancy clothes, vacations, and a large bank account. Is that the truth? Is that what makes us happy? To continue, consuming high cholesterol beef and chicken containing saturated fat to give us protein or to drink milk for healthy bones. Is that the truth? Is everything a facade? Is everything designed for you to spend money on big industry and in debt to keep you working to pay for all the big government programs? Is everything designed to give you a chronic disease, so you visit doctors and take pills for the rest of your life made by some large pharmaceutical company? I bet you never looked at life that way; you just did what everyone else was doing. That's the dark side of the world. How does all of this and your ego affect you individually as a person?

Extinguishing the ego is about boundaries and personal power. It's about health, diet, mind, body, and soul. It's about doing and thinking the right thing. When we're not practicing boundaries in all facets of life, we often lose ourselves and our power. We are oblivious to the obvious. We lose sight of the big picture of life. We forget we are a spirit living in the flesh on a planet floating around in space. We forget how precious life is. We are pulled by our thoughts into the past and do not even realize it. We eat a poor diet and wonder why we are overweight and have a chronic disease. Then we allow some unconscious belief to guide us through. We follow others' advice and believe as they believe without doing the research. We go down the path of life and wonder why it seems so difficult. What is my purpose? What am I doing here on this planet, and why am I so sick? Why do some of my relationships fail? We allow the external world and our ego to influence us on so many levels. We do not even know whether they are correct or not. That is the "ego" that portrays our personality, guides our life, and attracts our happiness or pain.

There will come a time in everyone's life that we must choose what is right instead of taking the easy route. Life at the core is about doing the right thing all the time. There is an old Hawaiian word, Kina 'olé: Doing the right thing, in the right way, at the right time, in the right place, for the right individual, for the right reason, with the right feeling, the first time. It's about removing your negative ego to experience a life filled with love, joy, and memories. It's about removing your version of life and replacing it with the truth about yourself and everything around you to open the endless possibilities of the universe. It's about helping others and bringing joy to all we love. It's about being healthy and happy. However, the ego of humans can create incredible drama in our lives. Some people just see life differently and believe the world revolves around them. It's a journey to let go of the ego to end the drama of one's life.

Many times, the people closest to us, hurt us the most. They see us in a different light than others. They treat us differently. They have known us since we were young, immature, made mistakes, or struggled to make sense of our life. We were in trouble at school, on a substance, or failed in some endeavor. They think our ideas are way off track or we are off course. We, too, have that same behavior with our friends, children, or people at work. We judge them. That is the ego. We must instead plant the seed in people's hearts and our own heart that we all have a purpose. We must be patient and allow the seed to take root. Everyone is on a journey. The universe waits to reach our destiny; our job is to enable the seed to grow. We must not rush it. We must learn to use love instead of our ego to be the guiding light. We must give ourselves and others the time and space to understand the seed for themselves. That is the circle of the ego.

The ego can create such darkness and evil inside you. Unless you travel within yourself, you may never see this in your life.

It is the voice that creates separation between us and anything suitable in our lives.

It tells us we do not deserve to be happy or loved.

It traps us in the shame or guilt of the past and fear of the future.

It says, poor me when something does not go our way.

It adds drama and fear of anything negative or something that we do not know.

It is easily offended, angry, and jealous.

It lives by the flesh and desires.

It is unkind to people because your mother/father/brother/sister was unkind.

It argues with your spouse because your parents argued.

It destroys future relationships because your husband/wife left you.

It destroys you due to an unloving parent.

It always thinks of themselves first and is always right.

It blames others for making you unhappy then wants the other person to fix the unhappiness.

 That is the ego madness many people live these days. Is that you? I hope not; however, you can only change you. It's tough to erase your ego. I get it. Your experiences of life build the ego. The ego becomes your defense mechanism. An unchecked ego can develop into unconscious behaviors that one never sees. A toxic ego can destroy people. Only by traveling through the inner journey of love can the toxic ego be erased. When you release the ego, the whole world around you will change.
 As humans, we all want to be loved in a specific way; however, human love is not absolute; it has conditions attached to it. However, when one lives by their spirit, they allow love to become the overall motive for their actions and words. They enable their soul to lead them. They allow the spirit to bring love and abundance into their lives. They enable the universe to bring them wisdom to let go of the past and to love others

without conditions. They embrace all facets of life; the good and the bad. They connect with the universe's unconditional love and spread that love.

The spirit destroys the ego by demonstrating love to ourselves and the world. The less ego we have, the more we avoid tough things in life. We let life unfold before us, and we engage with what is and not what we want it to be. We quit attempting to fill in the puzzle piece that does not fit. We stop trying to shove the piece into our lives. We find the part that fits and brings us joy. We allow life to flow and understand everything that happens to us happens for a reason. We know the soul is always guiding us to learn the lesson of unconditional love for ourselves. We understand everything is a lesson and not let our ego lead us into the darkness of despair. We accept the outcome of all life events.

The spirit leads one to become humble, kind, giving, compassionate, honest, peaceful, open, and loving. The soul always wants harmony with people, and the understanding that life is about love and balance.

It is the belief that the universe is in control, not us.

It frees us from the past and future and gives us the ability to live in the now.

It anchors love in all our motives.

It spreads peace in all communications.

It sets boundaries and oversees our relationships and emotions, so we do not fall prey to the negativity of the world or feel betrayed.

It brings back personal power and guides us to our path of growth.

It brings ownership to our emotions and keeps one's mistakes on their side of the road.

It brings accountability to oneself by how we treat ourselves and others.

It brings reality into view with no need to change anything or anyone.

It gives us the knowledge that we only need to change ourselves.

It lifts one out of the dark times.

It understands everything happens for a reason to learn a lesson.

It guides one to the understanding of how beautiful their life is.

It releases all pain and leads one to bring hope to all beings.

It leads to peace.

It leads one to understand the foundation of life is love.

It spreads light into the dark world.

It releases one to the belief that anything is attainable in this lifetime.

 The spirit leads one to the meaning of life, love, and the love of others. When you live by the spirit's voice, you are no longer a victim or feel betrayed by anything and live with love for yourself and all living creatures.

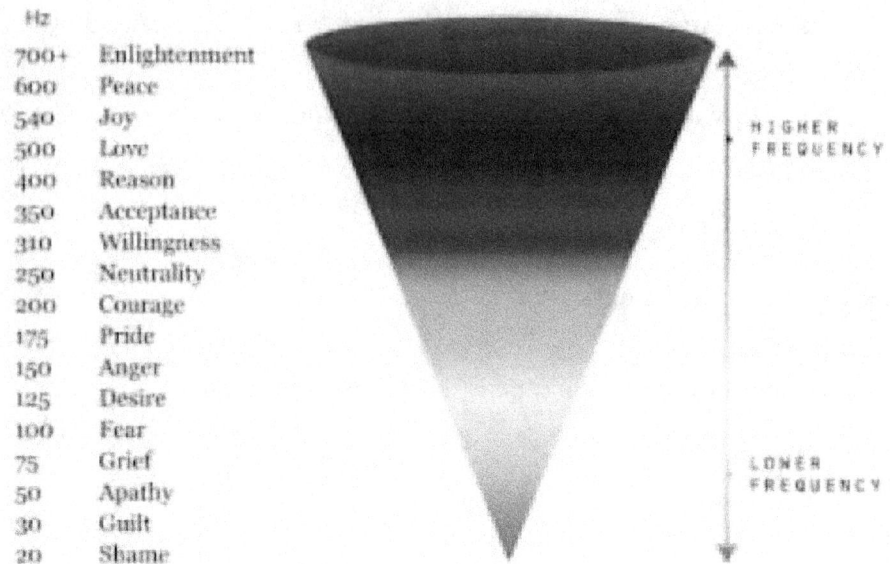

VIBRATION

"Vibrate at the highest frequency possible."
– The Universe

We all have this energy source within us, an electricity, a vibration that permeates our minds, hearts, and souls. We are made up of different energy levels: emotional, physical, mental, and spiritual. Each energy has a vibration and combines to create the overall vibrational frequency of a being. Everything in the universe vibrates at one frequency or another: a tree, an animal, a human, a vehicle, everything. We're like a radio station sending out our frequency. It's the connection to all living things and the force within us that emits our feelings to others.

The universe is a fractal to help you understand yourself better and works with the inner self to help you experience the outer. Everything in the world vibrates at one speed or another and is attracted to the same. The vibration is created by the inner thoughts, emotions, and external actions of the being. All our thoughts are on a particular wave and attract what we are sending out. For example, saying hello to someone with a smile or showing them, some form of kindness will raise yours and their vibration should they respond in some affirmative manner. Our emotions also vibrate at a certain level as we have all felt something beautiful or off. You hear it all the time when someone says, "I get a bad vibe around them, or that place has a good vibe." For example, when you are in line at the grocery store or somewhere in public and someone walks up behind you. You get a gut feeling that they are either good, bad, a threat, upset, happy, and on and on. And our actions also vibrate at a certain level. For example, when you hold a door open for a person, depending on your strategic location, the person behind you will do the same for someone else. That action becomes contagious and attracts more energy. Like a football or baseball team, someone has a big play or hits a home run, everybody gets pumped, even the people watching it on television. The collective yelling or moaning during or after the event is everyone's vibration joining as one. People singing together at a concert is everyone's vibration coming together as a single voice, that's the energy. That is the connection. Be aware this power exists in you, and when you use it wisely, you can attract and attain endless possibilities in your life.

We attract what we are on the inside or what we think about ourselves and where our life is headed. We should strive every day to manifest our life, channel our energy to accomplish our goals. To seek goodness within, pursue our dreams, do good things for others, and act right as good is the universe working through us. When we do good things, our energy builds at a high frequency, and we illuminate positive qualities such as love, tolerance, respect, compassion, forgiveness, and happiness. The positive energy created acts like a magnet to attract the same in return for us. We open to a new avenue, recognize the universe's plan, and release the perceived control. We become whole and live in harmony and balance at all levels of our minds, bodies, and souls. That, in turn, builds our vibration and attracts what we seek.

There is also a mirror of life that also attracts what needs to be healed inside us, like self-betrayal, not telling the truth, self-abandonment, loneliness, shame, guilt, etc. Our soul then guides us through our journey and acts as a magnet to attract those relationships with the hope of healing ourselves. As we go through our daily routines, these attractions often reflect unconscious patterns of dark habits. They rear their ugly head from our desire to experience love. It's the vibration of the soul that is the conduit to attract the relationships to find self-love, love of others, and meaning.

When we use the thoughts of love and forgiveness to heal ourselves from the things that are disconnected or damaging to our soul, it allows us to live in the present moment and recognize the beauty of ourselves, others and the world around us. We understand the unique charm of everything the way it is and learn to accept it and love it. For example, when you go to someone's house, and think they should move their furniture around or have a different color of carpet or tile. You may say something and then wonder why they never invite you over again. Instead, allow people to be people. Release the control in your mind and enjoy the moment. Accept in your consciousness that you are not always right.

When you raise your vibration, you will become empowered and attract the positive experiences you crave. We all want things to change overnight; however, that's not how it works. Sometimes the gain, the growth, takes years. You must remain faithful. And you will still experience hardships, betrayals, and failures; it will not be perfect. However, by continuing these actions that keep your vibration high, your soul will guide you to do the right thing and overcome these obstacles. You will attract people and experiences to what you are spending your energy thinking about. You will slowly realize that you are the person in control of your thoughts and destiny. That is the path to become who and what you want to be.

Like snowflakes, there are no two souls alike. Recognize how incredibly unique you are. Your overall vibration is the direct reflection of your emotions, inner thoughts, beliefs, health, choice of words, view of the Earth, and others. As only light bleeds out dark, strive to do the tough mental work within to remove the darkness from your mind, body, and soul. Like a painter using light colors to brighten the dark tones of the canvas, the more love you use, the higher your vibration and the more light you hold. The higher your consciousness, the more you are connected to your soul and the universe.

When we become aware and set out to heal, balance, and activate these thoughts, we unify ourselves with our physical body. Although we identify ourselves as flesh and skin, we are merely energy, every thought, feeling, and action is. By understanding this, you invite in a divine plan and usher in a new outlook on life. You recognize the beauty of the self. You realize the power resides in yourself as we are all spiritual beings on a journey to heal whatever is destroying our soul. Sit back and comprehend the lessons when they present themselves and shine a light on them. Understand this is not a smooth ride; however, when you have removed the dark from your soul and replaced it with the view of love, you understand your vibration and the true meaning of your life and being alive. You are not bound, and whatever abundance you create with your mind is attainable. You understand life is about love, people, and the love of people.

Living by the vibration of love gives you the understanding that love is the absence of fear, is the fire of our passions, lifts our limitations in life, is our spirit, and is the essence of the universe. Love is the understanding of why we are even here and alive. Love is hidden in plain sight, is the law of life, is the law of the universe, and the law of attraction. Live to recognize and accept the gifts of the universe. Allow the love to fill your life with a sense of peace and accomplishment within your mind, body, and soul. Live in the love vibration.

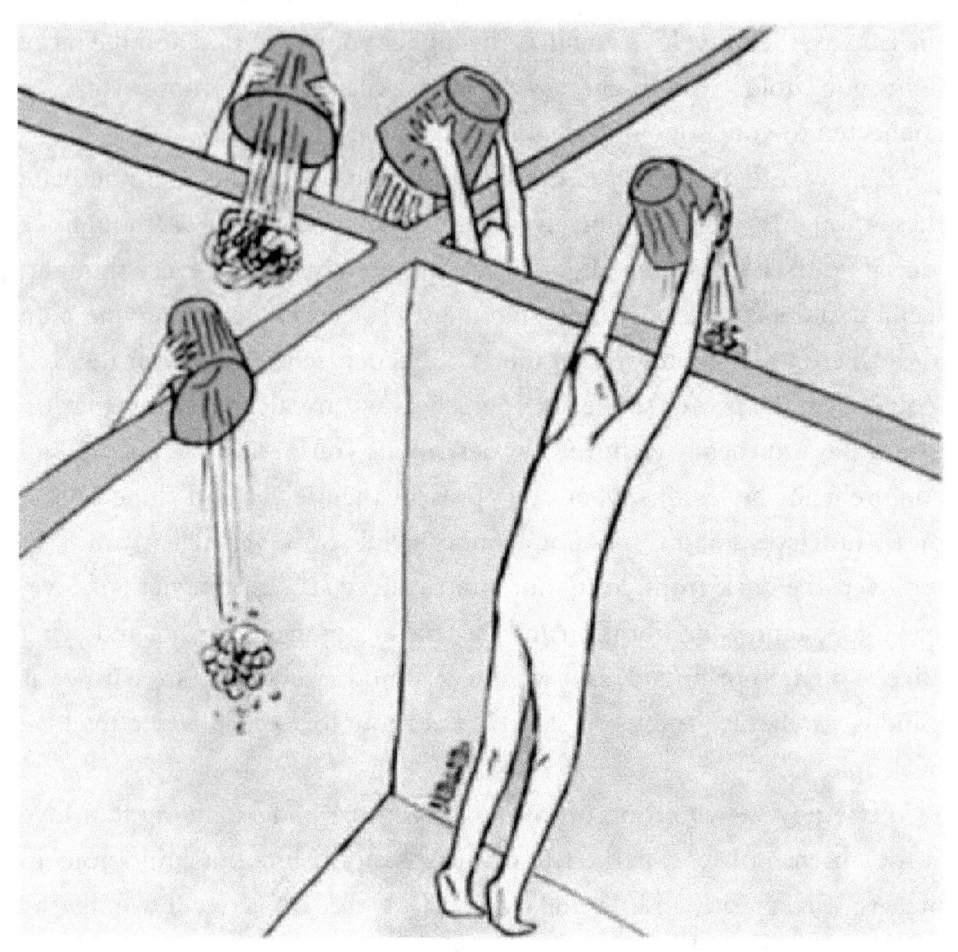

Karma

"How people treat you is their karma; how you react is yours."
– Wayne Dyer

Karma is defined in Hinduism and Buddhism as the sum of a person's actions in this and previous states of existence, viewed as deciding their fate in future lives. Karma in the western world is defined as destiny or fate, following as effect from a cause. Meaning, how you treat people, hurt them, or steal from them, for example, is what will happen to you in return so that you can experience the pain. To further, should you beat dogs, you will come back as a dog to experience all the pain you inflicted. However, karma is much deeper and more significant than that. When you realize the evolution of a spiritual being, you are a spirit having a human existence, is when you crossover and leave your ego behind and open to what karma is.

Most people today operate in the 3D world, the ego of the flesh, and mundane things. All things external. Every situation you encounter in life is the result of karma. Very few people will realize how many of their desires are generated by karma. They believe this is free will; however, they are acting out of their buried desires in their subconscious. When you move on to what is termed a 4D experience outside your subconscious and recognize that your existence is way bigger, internal, and a lesson is when you comprehend karma. You understand your present life is designed as an inner journey to self-love and heal all past events. According to some, should you not take personal responsibility for the self to heal, you will repeatedly incarnate until you do. Let's dive in and scratch the surface so you get some form of understanding that karma may not be what you have done in this lifetime; it may be the accumulation of what your soul has done through its existence.

The karma beliefs of human beings are a direct collision between spirituality, religion, and faith. The religious teachings of the world, humankind, teach either we have one lifetime or many lifetimes to become whole, pure, compassionate, joyful, and find love within ourselves to reach salvation. I am in no way suggesting that you believe a certain way here, that's strictly up to you. To add to the equation, perhaps when we hear the phrase "Go to the Light," when you pass away, your soul is reborn into a hospital room, and you cry because you realize you still have lessons to learn. Oh, the pain. At this point, we don't know, however, whatever you believe, some things are unexplainable, like some events in your life.

At a certain point in one's life, the entity's spiritual energy is ready, and a set of circumstances will happen to trigger the flooding of the accumulated suffering over their entire existence. For example, someone on their deathbed, someone diagnosed with cancer, someone with a near-death experience, a romantic breakup, or the loss of a loved one. The person within their consciousness will ask themselves, "What have I done?" The flood gates will open. All the past suffering rises to the surface, and they will have to address it. They will be led by their spirit to heal by reaching out to people, children, relatives, anyone they have done wrong, and apologize. The being will then be led by their inner voice to shed light, love, on the darkness, and understand "the lessons" of this lifetime.

Most people, however, live in the 3D world. The world of subconscious and awareness is about things. Their thoughts are about external things; wealth and material possessions, reputation, marital and sexual status, beauty, social status, power, money, greed, etc. Their value is from such things, what I own, what others think of me and what I can do, look at me, look at me. However, should they fail to acquire these things, they will consider people will see them as weak, dumb, or a loser. Then they go down the trail of negative thought and live in the past and question their every move. The dangers will present themselves everywhere and wherever they go. They can never lower their guard and relax. Life becomes a never-ending competition for survival, prosperity, and a need to prove themselves. Who can attract the prettiest mate, wife, husband, or possess the most beautiful house, cars, boats, boobs, job, clothes, etc…? They never escape this world; it lasts their entire lifetime, and they are never happy because they chase their ego until they die. They never step back and become grateful for what they have; they just want to consume like a locust. That is why you see so many unhappy people in the world these days that won't even respond when you simply say hello. They never step back and realize how blessed they are; they worry about what they do not have. The 3D world is shallow, swim to the deep end of the pool; you will find another reality and joy.

When you do have some defining moment in your life that leads you to the understanding that you are a spirit that flesh surrounds, you understand the value of love and people. You know the world is more significant than your wallet. You start to question your spirituality, what you stand for, and where your life is headed. You cross over to the consciousness of spirituality. You understand the sacred nature of people, life, souls, and existence itself. In your gut, you feel how critical emotions and how other people's choices affect their journey. You understand that all actions that have caused suffering, pain, separation, and negativity are inflicted on the self. The mirror comes into play, as all external reality reflects the inner self. Every harmful action that causes some type of pain will forever carry that same pain within its spiritual self. That is the "karma." The energy of negative effect towards others motivated by negativity and self-interest, accumulated within the person. That energy is tied to the spiritual lessons of the current lifetime.

Ultimately, each being's lessons and karma are internal, inside one's self. The teachings of the lifetime are the responsibility of the soul. When all the pain associated with past actions to others now rises to the surface, the previous hurtful actions need to be solved. It's all about restoring balance to the self. The soul knows what needs to re-integrated and what lessons need to be learned. One must look inside and stop the blame game of others or the world, causing their struggles. Once the lessons are addressed, the separation of the pain held over a long time can heal. The energy and the connection to others, empathy, can now be felt. Compassion and forgiveness of self begin to develop, and the journey of self begins.

Like the universe and all of nature, which is in balance, people are out of balance. When we understand our lessons, we come into balance and raise our vibration. By following our karma, we know our journey, and we appreciate our life. By integrating our soul and karma, we heal our inner pain and suffering. Once we have accomplished and understood karma lessons, all the guilt, shame, and self-pity would have no place to live inside us.

Karma is also a present force, an energy vortex connected to an event in our life. We all have thoughts about ourselves and others every day. We ponder our past and relationships at home, work, on the road, and in public. And many of us have been divorced, or had an unloving mother or father, a lousy grandparent, an angry sibling, a troubled child, participated in unhealthy relationships, and lost many friends over our lifetime. When we carry this associated energy inside us like fear, anger, shame, or guilt and feel the emotion when we have these thoughts, we are giving the idea "karma" energy. Anything we give energy to will attract what we are thinking. These thoughts become our subconscious and affect everything we think about. It attracts relationships with the hope of healing ourselves of the pain. However, when we learn to forgive others and ourselves of these events, we release energy and karma. We become balanced. We do not react with the negative internal energy anymore to the thought, and it doesn't hurt anymore.

How do we know when the "karma" is finished and learned the lesson or healed?

You will know once a karmic event or action is no longer in your daily thoughts. You won't think about the activity or person anymore, and you are not caught up in the energy of it when you do. The energy and emotion have been dissipated. It has escaped your awareness, and you feel free—for example, a romantic breakup, divorce, or loss of a loved one. You twirl around in mind about all kinds of energy (actions, words, emotions) for some time. Wondering about them and how they felt, or you felt. Then over a period, one day, you find yourself thinking, "I haven't had that thought in a while." Then, wow, and I do not feel the hurt or emotion anymore. Karma is an energy vortex revolving around a particular action or thought. When you dissolve the energy associated with that specific energy vortex, you dissolve the karma. You become free to use your energy doing and thinking about things that bring joy to your life and others. You forgive yourself and others. You create beautiful memories instead of attracting drama to your life. You have come a step closer to loving yourself unconditionally.

THE FOUNDATION OF LIFE

"Humility is the solid foundation of all virtues."
– Confucious

A foundation is an underlying basis or principle for something or the lowest-bearing part of a building. When applying to life, the understanding and building block of life. Life is a mystery to most; however, when you understand balance, respect, trust, boundaries, expectations, and love, you can build any foundation. The foundation of love is one of joy, love, and trust, of course, there are many other factors; however, these are the core. When you build a foundation of life based on love, things expand exponentially. Understanding that your life has a meaning, and we are all here for a reason is when you know your journey. We are all on a quest to find loving relationships on all levels and find love for ourselves. Sometimes it takes an event for us to question our lives, and sometimes people have an innate thirst and figure it without something happening. Whichever way, when we hurt inside, our soul is crying out to be healed from past emotions that are out of balance with the universe. The private lesson is to harbor it or let it go. We must then find the balance within ourselves to release the pain and find joy in our lives. That understanding allows us to recognize our lessons and build the foundation to understand it.

All of us will experience an event or several in life to cause us to go soul searching. This event, when paid attention to and understood, will lead one to the inner self, or one will be too fearful to look within at the root cause of the pain and get stuck in life. Consume substances, alcohol, become angry, stay in dysfunctional relationships, stay at a terrible job, many negative things. One then makes excuses to live their life on the negative side. They use these excuses to justify their bad behavior towards others and themselves. They choose to live this way. However, when we do pay attention and look within, it is when the healing begins. Life is about the inner-self and healing the inner self. Once we start to do this, we are on our way to no longer being the prisoner and to freedom.

When one becomes free, they understand that the external world is not at fault. Everything is not someone else's fault; however, sometimes it is. Bad things happen so that good things can be born from the ashes. We all need to learn to take responsibility for our actions. I am not saying that should someone pull out and hit your car just to blame yourself. I am saying that should you not do your homework or study and fail a class; it's not your teacher's fault. It's your fault. You may not believe this; we blame others for things because we want to project how we choose to live on the inside. We set them up to project our bad feelings into them. It's the mirror of life. The foundation is to start taking responsibility for our words and actions. And to forgive the words and actions of others.

We all live in a realm of duality and learn from people who are converse from us. People are different and raised differently. That's how you learn. Most people do not realize we are being led by our soul to self-love to find what we do not love ourselves. We are given opportunities to love what we have rejected within ourselves and attracted to relationships as a mirror of our subconscious self. We then confuse and disappoint ourselves along the way by the connections our soul desires. These are the relationships that push our buttons and cause us to go soul-searching. They are leading us to wholeness by triggering what needs to be healed inside us. One is then attracted repeatedly to the same type of relationships to teach those lessons and heal those wounds. Until they are treated, a new teacher will show up again and again until they are. Once we do heal those wounds, we learn to love ourselves with our thoughts and actions.

It's easier to be a victim and justify psychotic behavior than to be happy. When we learn to forgive everything, we go through a spiritual cleansing and move to higher consciousness. We leave behind all the distractions and drama of the 3D world. We leave behind anything negative that does not provide growth. We understand our egoic voice has tripped us up to our entire life and blocked the gifts of the universe. We are then led by that voice to spread love and dispel the fears. We understand the universal rules of this planet and that the universe provided our whole existence, and we give thanks every day. We begin treating people the way we want to be treated. We understand the principle, we are not better than anyone else; however, we are not below anyone else. We understand our soul is our value, not the worldly things, not our job, not our marital or sexual status and not our ideology.

One's life meaning has been planned out before they were even conscious of this lifetime. It was a pact their soul made with others, soul family members, soul groups, and karmic partners. I know what you are thinking, what the hell? Is he crazy? These pacts are what transpires during your lifetime to get you back on track to finding your life's purpose. One must pay attention to understand that every event and hardship is the path to your life's meaning. These events may not have played out for you yet, so when they do, be aware and understand the track and the tests. Should you sit in despair when these events occur, you will never realize it and will never learn the lessons.

Once you surrender to this belief and believe in yourself, forgive yourself, and, most importantly, love yourself, things change, your whole life will change. Love and the abundance of the universe will surround you. The process brings all that has been inside you, the spirit's voice, into clarity. It is compelling and amazing that one's love of self and the love of the universe then understand the foundation of their journey. Love and forgiveness are the foundation; it's the lessons of the ego that are under constant construction to one's meaning and happiness. And it's the soul that connects, guides, and acts as a bridge across the foundation.

THE UNIVERSE

"The universe and we are the same"
– Anonymous

The universe is in perfect balance, all-powerful, and has endless energy and possibilities. Absolute abundance. It consists of fifty billion trillion stars, and they are just the right distance for our galaxy to exist in complete harmony, to a certain extent, as it does. It's a hidden vibratory field that connects us all. It has been called Akasha, Logos, the Higgs Boson, dark matter, and many other names. Many have stated it's the connection to the inner and outer worlds of beings. It exists for our earth and every living thing that surrounds us. The trees, animals, bugs, fish, birds, people, spirits, souls, space, etc. Look up some time; you may be amazed at the beauty instead of always staring at your smartphone.

The universe is the precise size and physics to sustain humans. Should it be smaller, only Hydrogen and Helium would exist, should it be more massive, only elements heavier than iron would exist. The perfect size to create carbon, oxygen, and nitrogen, the building blocks of life. There is such fine-tuning at all scales of the universe. If you change the expansion rate a fraction, there is no life. Every component, every event plays a critical role in our lives and the understanding that something out there must care about us. When one connects, it leads us to a higher power with respect and with a clear conscious. We understand that we all come from the same speck of dust that exploded billions of years ago. We are all the same elements; however, the mind is what makes us different.

That is the journey that allows one to speak, receive, and conjure the love of the universe into their thoughts. This knowledge empowers one's specific manifestations to become a reality. The universe provides what you ask from it. It's an invisible force that works when you ask for help or answers. There is a reason why people pray, to receive what they desire to achieve in life. Sending requests to the universe will be accepted. We all experience a time when you have someone on your mind, and then suddenly you receive a message, or they call you. It's the law of attraction and how the universe works. Put your dreams out into the world and believe. Focused energy is the most potent tool the universe has given to us—the real emotions for yourself and others inside your heart and mind. You are the "U" in the universe. When you believe in yourself, love yourself and manifest your life with loving thoughts, the universe will reward you in mysterious, beautiful ways.

Everything is vibrational frequency. The universe connects us all. It provides us the energy and knowledge to do anything we believe in ourselves we can do. It's a giant brain that is continually thinking. An invisible nervous system using hidden energy. Akashic Records, the matrix of energy, vibration, and infinite knowledge. It's up to us to unlock the experience that is already inside of us as it was for Leonardo DaVinci, Albert Einstein, and Nikola Tesla. However, when you have negative thoughts about life, others, and yourself, this shuts out the universe's abundance.

When I am having a bad day or experiencing unwanted thoughts or some form of being down, I always think back to three things that change my perspective. One is that we are floating around on a big rock in the middle of space; another is that I am lucky even to be alive, and the last, however not the least, is that I know there is a higher power above that loves me unconditionally. Let me explain so we can figure this out.

We are on what is called Earth, Mother Earth, which provides us everything we need to live through nature. How did we get here? I would like to figure that out one day, however, why does it matter? We are here now and living. Just think for a minute how big the universe is, and we are here on this minute part of it on a planet doing all the things we are doing. The earth consists of the ecosystems, the cities, the moon, the stars, the oceans, the lakes, the rivers, the mountains, the valleys, and everything that surrounds you. As long as we do not destroy it, this place is perfect. It consists of the smallest organism that is eaten by a bigger one and on and on. Those organisms excrete waste, and that somehow turns into dirt or fertilizer for something else to grow. We breathe air, and plants convert our exhales back into oxygen. We have seasons, four seasons a year in some places and less in others. The seasons bring life and death; however, they always bring a renewal of some form. The seasons are created by the earth's tilt, how the heck did that happen, to do things like trees to lose leaves, turtles to swim two-thousand miles to lay eggs, plants to bloom and animals to give birth. It's beautiful. So why do some of us not enjoy and understand the universe? Why do we go somewhere beautiful with people with false expectations and are bummed out? Why do we not enjoy beauty? Why do we stray away from love? Why are we so unhappy these days in life?

We all get caught up and lose track of ourselves and the lives of people we love—work, bills, relationships, television, politics, social media, smartphones, etc. We get disconnected from the overall purpose of our lives, and we are somewhat lost. We get in a rut and not excited about our future. We believe the external is supposed to bring us happiness; TVs, cars, trucks, beauty products, tattoos, houses, etc.… When they do not, we begin thinking evil thoughts and things start to spiral. Then our thoughts attract all the doom and gloom. For example, I bought a new car and let's say I must go to the grocery store; a parking lot. I like and pay for this car, so I do not want it to get dinged up or damaged. I am thinking this when I pull into the parking lot. I find a spot I think will be either way out of the way or a prominent place somewhere to be protected. I return, and someone has parked almost right next to me and dinged my car, or someone did not put their cart up, and it rolled into the side. Those negative thoughts attract negative actions from the universe. That is how the universe works. Instead, train yourself always to be thinking positive thoughts.

I am unsure why, however, I feel lucky all the time. Someone once told me, "The more I practice, the luckier I get." Imagine that. I have had some great life experiences and will continue to have them; I'm positive. Things in life do not just happen as everything happens for a reason, to teach a lesson, learn a lesson, or to let go of something damaging to your soul. Some people call this coincidence, which I do not believe in; however, there are circumstances. There is a fine line between coincidence and fate. Coincidence is a blessing that should you recognize it, brings someone or something into your life to help you to your meaning.

You are the director of your life movie with your thoughts. When you show up anywhere, you are there for a reason, recognize it. Attempt to end the process that you are somewhere, and my life is annoying because I must go somewhere with someone. Instead, say hello to someone. Have some fun while you are there. Recognize all the events and decisions since the beginning of time that had to happen for you to be alive and with the people surrounding you. You will be surprised by how the situation changes.

When I was five years old, there used to be this sporting goods store in the area where I grew up. My father used to go up there a lot and take my older brothers. One day they had this contest to give away a new rod and reel. My dad signed up my five, and seven-year older brothers. You had to cast this three-ounce weight about thirty-five yards into a yellow inflatable raft. It was about seven feet long and three feet wide. They threw, and nobody won. So, I'm at home, minding my own business, which I have pretty much done my entire life, and in comes my dad and brothers. He says, "We are going up to the store." We get there, and he says, "There is this contest, and I'm signing you up." I get out there and throw the deal, without practice, and miss, however, I felt something inside me to correct the issue. On the second cast, I nailed it, won the rod-and-reel, and we drove home. Father very proud, brothers angry, meaning you know how brothers are.

About six weeks later, we traveled to the Texas Coast to fish as we always did for our annual summer vacation. We were out wade fishing (walking in the water with our poles, bait bucket, and net), and my brothers took off, and I hung with my dad as the water was about up to my shoulders. On the first cast, I threw this shrimp right into this cut along a reef. BOOM. I ended up fighting this twenty-two-inch redfish for twenty minutes, yelling, "Dad, Dad, take this pole and get him," all he said in a calm voice: "That's your pole and your fish, you get him." I continued, and my dad netted the fish for me. It was the most prominent and only fish of the day. My brothers, again angry.

What happened is that I visualized that fish. Every time I went hunting or fishing when I was a kid, I always did that every time, and I was very successful. That is what you need to do in your life to connect with your thoughts to become a reality. Visualize what you want your life to be fully and expend thought energy towards it. I allowed fearful subconscious thoughts to get in the way when I was older. When you have doubt, fear, and let things bother you, you are blocking the universe. You are turning off the faucet of abundance. You are attracting the negative. You must fully believe in the right thoughts as the universe knows when you have not bought in all the way. Buy in, feel it, and in yourself. Once you have bought in, you will see the world around you and your life change like the seasons. Stay in the season of renewal and growth always. Then you have connected to the vibration of the universe.

I have always believed in a higher power. You may call this God, the universe, ancient aliens, a higher power, or many other names. I never took the time to read the entire religious books most of you know. Or sit back and think about what's up there or why or how I'm connected. I have my thoughts; however, whatever you believe is up to you. The night my brother passed away, several events I witnessed screamed out to me one day when I reflected. I was sitting at a friend's place talking, and the subject came up out of nowhere and asked what had happened. She had a son that had passed away, so we had a connection to this stuff. As I told her, all these memories flooded in. I left an hour or so later and thought about that fateful night over the next few days when I was writing.

The story goes like this. I remembered that we received a call a little after two AM, and my parents left for the hospital shortly after. I stayed home with my Siamese cat; her name was DD. She was lying on my bed with me. About four AM, she began to rub on me and meow, like she wanted me to let her out. At this point, my parents were still at the hospital, so I got up, and she led me to our front door. I thought that's strange as she usually went out the side door through the kitchen to the garage. A feeling inside made me look out our front door with a semi-circle at the top with four small triangle windows. You can see this lighted main road across a field about a quarter to a half-mile; it looked like a lighted racetrack. I looked outside, and at the same time, a tow truck with my brother's truck behind it came by. I watched the wrecked vehicle until it passed at the bottom of our street under the streetlights. I was stunned at the damage. I knew right away that my brother had passed away. I prayed he had not passed; however, that feeling was too strong to fight. I looked down at my cat, and she stared straight into my eyes and had this look that still makes me think she was someone or something else.

Move forward, and my parents came home and told me the news. We all laid in bed. I could hear my mother crying, and my dad calls my eldest brother to inform him. I tossed and turned for hours as I couldn't sleep. I had a baseball game that morning and decided to go instead of staying home in utter despair. It happened to be April first, April Fool's Day. I picked up my buddy on the way to school, and he said what the heck is up. I told him and said not to tell anyone yet as I am not ready, and the conversation fell silent. We arrived at school, and I gathered my equipment and jumped on the bus.

On the way to the stadium, I stared at the beautiful sunny sky with white clouds floating by looking for my brother with tears. We get to the ballpark, and I warm up. Another guy was pitching that day, so I take a spot on the bench. We played against a school that my brother disliked when he was in school, coincidence? About four warmup throws in; our pitcher throws out his back. My coach tells me to get out there and get warmed up. I had not spoken to anyone about my brother except my buddy, so no one knew. I get out there and warm up for as long as I need as this is an injury time out, and the rules allow it. I warm up for about eight minutes, tip my hat and tell them I am ready.

At that time, the announcer comes on the PA system and announces me as my brother, my brother's name, the one that passed away earlier that morning. My brother never played baseball; he had been out of school for four years and was not associated with the team in any fashion except to watch me play when he could. At the same time, my eldest brother from Dallas, Texas, and my dad arrive at the stadium. My brother hears this and goes up to the announcer and tells him my name, and he announces it correctly. Now I am seventeen years old, on the pitching mound in the middle of everything and experience this. I didn't think about it. I did not have the time. I was starting a game and had to be in that frame of mind. I pitched five innings, and we won. After the game, when I was walking to the bus, I asked myself, was that my brother saying goodbye? Was that the higher power? Am I crazy? I understand now as an adult; I will let you make your own decision on what you think. The higher power works in mysterious ways, remember that!

The universe does not move to your wants; you must release the perceived control and line yourself up with the world's balance. I had a guy stop by my desk one day at work, and he saw that I had over attained my quota and happened to have it up on the screen. I am in sales. He said, "You must be living right." I said, "You bet and having fun doing it." He said, "I bet the fun started when you saw this." I said, "No, I had fun way before this." He then said, "How is it that you are always having fun?" I said that I had connected to the universe and used love to solve my internal and external issues. He then asked a random question as to why someone who lost their leg in an accident, using positive thought and reaching out to the universe, does not receive a new appendage. A flesh and blood leg. Or why anyone has never seen the higher power. I was a little struck; however, I told him, we will never see the higher power, his love works through the actions and words of others.

Should a person be a positive person who has faith, vital, and visualize a new leg and surround themselves with people who love and care about them, they will receive a prosthetic leg, rehabilitation and be on a different path in life. The universe helps those who help themselves. This setback is just another fork in the road of their journey. He then said, isn't that the community. I said that is a part of it; it's the universe working through the community using love to get this person down their path of life. You never know what this leads to, a new passion, a new job, a new mission, you never know. He walked off, still convinced the power of love does not exist. That's his journey to find out and to find happiness the universe wants your life to be.

We all came from the same speck of dust that exploded billions of years ago. When you show others through giving, loving, and forgiving, you are demonstrating the universe. You are creating love through your consciousness. However, there is evil in the world working through others as well. And we sometimes carry the heavy burden of trapped emotions inside us and allow that energy to run our life. Trust me; you are not the only one in this world that has experienced unwanted events. We all have issues and crosses to bear. It takes courage to begin the process of separating yourself and others' dark thoughts to forgiveness of both. Learn to let go and steer your life this way.

When you have thoughts that you are lonely, sad, and think nobody loves you, remember, you have a higher power out there that does, unconditionally, and hopefully yourself. That's two, all the time. We are all separated from the universe when we were born as our souls separated from the source. Your separation thoughts in life are a test to bring you back to "The Source," the creator, and to stop only thinking about yourself. So, stop beating yourself up and upset that you are alone. Take the time to figure out what is driving those unwanted thoughts. Love will always find you when you show love to yourself and others. It may take some time, never give up.

The universe is a beautiful thing. It supplies all of us the elements to keep you alive, hit your senses, and the knowledge to read this book. Take some time, step back, and recognize that. Life is not a race; quit rushing through it, slow down, smell the roses, and absorb the beauty. Love the earth and all living things. Love yourself and all the people who surround you with love. Tell them you love them. Live, that's what you were put on this planet to do, to live it up! Put the smartphone down and forgive whoever did anything you perceive as wrong to you. Release the energy, so you stop spending time thinking about it. Do not be afraid to look within for the answers, conquer the fear and yourself. Enjoy your life! Don't miss out even on a Monday; it will screw up your whole week.

Connecting to the universe and all its power allows you to visualize and make your life's dreams come true. Fearful thoughts only hold you back. When you have an idea and think you do not have the money, or someone says, "That's stupid", do the research. Believe it, and you will come across a favored connection to help you. Then, put in the time to gain knowledge. Listen to your inner self. Believe in it, believe in yourself. You will attract the things that you are seeking, and you will have connected with the universe.

CONNECTING TO THE UNIVERSE

"When people go within and connect with themselves, they realize they are connected to the universe, and they are connected to all living things."
– Armand Dimele

I had an epiphany (Meditation), much like the three wise men from the East, and one day I started reaching out to every person I thought I had hurt that I could remember. I highly suggest you do this in your way. I began by telling my mother and father I loved them and thanked them for my upbringing (Gratitude) and being such great parents, which they were. I'm not saying tell someone who was not. Should that be the case, you must search for the wisdom to find forgiveness for them. I had no idea how good I had it after some stories I will mention in this book (Writing).

I should have told my parents' twenty-five years ago, but I was asleep at the wheel.

I began with old girlfriends and old friends. I scrolled through my phone and called about fifteen to twenty people. It was stunning the responses I received. I began by saying, "Hello, and how have you been?" The surprise! I let the conversation flow from there; I'm in sales. I preceded to tell them "I have changed myself; I'm not in some twelve-step program, I am doing this myself, and I am sorry should I have hurt you and want to apologize and ask for your forgiveness." Wow, the power and emotion. Most of them said they appreciated that and accepted my apology. I even met a few of them for drinks or dinner and talked.

I met up with a woman I had only briefly somewhat dated. We met at a restaurant and started talking and drinking, ordered some appetizers, and shared a small meal. Throughout the conversation, she never said a word about what had happened, although I was a jerk. I again apologized, and she said no need, I know you are a nice person. The night ended, I hugged her, and that was it. She still reaches out now and then to go out. Another woman I briefly dated pretty much said the same thing. I texted her and said, "I apologize for breaking up....I never meant to hurt you, and should I have, I am asking for your forgiveness." She said no need, I know you, and you are a nice person and a great friend. Again, it was all good; everything was clear. Even my ex-wife was surprised when I did the same with her. We ended up talking for forty-five minutes when I called. I was quite surprised. They all pretty much said thank you and how much better they felt about things now and seemed to let it all go. How did they feel? "Huh?", I said to myself. I cleared the proverbial air. What I did was clear myself out. I released the trapped negative emotional energy. I felt free.

I realized that everything happened just how it was supposed to be the person I am today. You can get stuck in life with past relationships, learn the lessons and change the tire, like a vehicle when you have a flat, and get down the road. When you reflect on yourself and show love for others, you are connecting to the universe. You are using the power of love and changing your vibrational attraction. You are displaying not only that you love yourself but also bringing closure and demonstrating love to that person. You are cleaning your clock and learning that life is not about material things; it's about love, people, and the people you love. Think about that!

Connecting with the universe is not about people. It's about connecting with all living things and with nature. You see and know people who connect with dogs, cats, horses, dolphins, monkeys; you name it. They connect through the universe by demonstrating love. When you express love for others and yourself, the energy connects you. Animals feel it, like people, and especially children. You will notice when you connect with people, they smile, laugh, have a good time, and no one is upset. The opposite is true when people are selfish, annoying, and mean. You have been there, and the result is not a good time. However, every experience is an adventure and an opportunity to learn and understand.

Learning to accept things and people as they are is a refreshing way to live. When you start practicing the art of not judging people, your whole life will change. These days, anyone can be offended or angry about anything. Some people have just not connected to the love of the universe or live in the past. The issues of greed, the breakdown of the family, the slow destruction of the education system, and the removal of a higher power from everything have caused many people worldwide to view life as dark. They are victims of some sort or hold on to painful life experiences. All the hardships you have faced are for a reason to learn something or to teach something. You never know what showing love to someone will do for them and how that guides them to the universe.

I was down in San Antonio, Texas, visiting my mother one day and took her to lunch. After lunch, we walked to the truck, and a girl in the parking lot approached us. I could tell she was a young, homeless, defeated woman. She asked for money, and I helped my mom into my vehicle. I pulled out my wallet and gave her fifteen dollars and said, life is tough, you can do anything with it, promise me one thing, "To do the right thing all the time." She said okay, thank you and hung her head. As she walked away, I said to be safe, and something came over me, my inner voice, to tell her, "I Love You." After I did, she popped around, lifted her head, smiled, and said, "like the higher power said, huh?" I said, "yes." I could see the energy build. Her whole face lit up. It was a fantastic sight and experience. She acted as though no one ever told her that in her life. She said, "I Love you too." Her whole demeanor changed. She walked away a different person with a smile and waved goodbye. Simply stunning. My mom said, "What happened out there?" I said, "I hope I changed that girl's life."

These actions show empathy. They demonstrate you can put yourself in someone else's shoes and understand the pain. That shows clarity of life. That shows you have crossed over and stopped caring only about yourself. Living this way will change your life for the better by allowing you to see the clarity of your journey. The journey is all about understanding your true self, your genuine thoughts, and your real emotions. When you know yourself, and what the essential things are that make you happy, you make all the people you surround yourself with happy. By using the principles of the higher power and demonstrating them to others, it changes lives. It changes your life! It connects you to the universe, which feeds energy and thoughts into your mind to fulfill your life. We then do not allow the dribble of today's (me me) culture to confuse us of this. By displaying love, the universe seeks you, rewards you, and ultimately guides you to the successful heights you aspire to be that live inside your thoughts.

Connect with these thoughts, and your world will change. Be like spring all the time, continually renewing yourself like a garden. When you take care of your plants, feed them, water them, talk to them, nourish them, show them love, what happens, they grow like crazy. That's what you need to do, feed your mind, body, and soul garden. That same process is how you connect to the universe. You show that same garden love to all the living things you interact with; you have uplifting thoughts about yourself and others. You live life to the fullest and do not judge people. When you keep feeding and putting your ideas out in the universe, they become a reality. When you believe and do the tough mental work, this will bring the positive things you desire in life and the people you love closer to you. It's not what you want out of life; it's about how much pain you must go through to get it. Once understood, you will have connected to the universe. The universe awaits you when you do.

Putting yourself out there for others or giving is one of the ultimate experiences of life. You must prepare for it; you must work for it. You must believe in yourself to fully comprehend it. Being selfish and allowing your ego or your pride to run your life will take away from the gifts of the universe. When you apply all the good things in life to yourself and others, the abundance of rewards you receive in return will bring love and hope into your heart. The act of caring for others more than yourself, empathy, is a trait that brings internal salvation. These thoughts and actions will connect you with the universe. You will feel the energy building inside you. Others will see the energy, and you displayed and understood that love could conquer anything, even yourself. The universe can giveth and taketh. Ensure you are on the right side of that, as the universe is all-powerful, once you tap in. Anything in your life is attainable. Find your connection.

CONSCIOUS VS. SUBCONSCIOUS MIND

"What we plant in our subconscious mind and nourish with repetition and emotion will become a reality."
– Earl Nightingale

Your conscious and subconscious mind are things one does not particularly think about in their lives. Unless one begins the process of learning how and why we act the way we do in life. External sources drive most of our thoughts; emotional memories, television, work, romantic partners, neighbors, parents, childhood, and so on. When we breakdown why we act or react in specific ways at a particular event in time, we realize ideas, values, and morals have been in our mind. We believe them and act on them no matter whether they are true or not. This behavior is what our parents or whoever raised us taught us. That is our subconscious mind, and what drives our life. Our conscious mind is how we react with our emotions to certain external situations using our subconscious beliefs. We could study this for years, but let's go over the basics to understand how to tap in and use each one wisely.

Your conscious mind is that part of our brain responsible for thinking, the external, the present. For example, talking, tasks, whatever we do when we are moving around and operating in life. Your conscious mind is what you associate with who you are and how you react to the outside world. It is responsible for logic and reasoning and filters out things that do not fit your belief system. For example, when you see someone and your mind races off to judge them. We all do this, and you think they are a loser or any other derogatory term we label each other. Instead of going down the path of judgment, you begin thinking that everyone has qualities, parents, and loved ones. You retrain your mind to see people differently, and you quit judging them. That belief then slowly, after much practice, begins moving to your subconscious. You start to live your life thinking this new belief and possibly that you are not better than anyone else. You are not below anyone else either, by the way. Your views on life have changed, and you open to a new way of thinking. That thought, or belief, then ultimately moves to your subconscious mind, and you no longer live life judging others.

To change a belief is to convince the conscious mind logically to accept it so that it can pass to the subconscious mind and reside there. Meaning, you must rewire your brain to let go of a belief. By retraining the intention to act in this manner to become spiritually mature, we allow ourselves to let go of all the unloving expectations in our subconscious mind and heal. We then can become balanced, so we have the ability, mentally, to show loving actions to others and ourselves. That's how we navigate through our subconscious beliefs with our conscious mind.

The subconscious mind operates in a dormant state when we are living by our conscious mind. When we learn or experience something in our conscious mind, it moves to our subconscious. For example, driving home from work, navigating through our local grocery store, or putting deodorant on in the morning, did I remember? That action becomes routine, and we are relaxed or do not have to pay such close attention. That same process is how we change the beliefs we know are out of balance with the universe to our subconscious mind.

Our subconscious is the place where our beliefs and memories are stored. It's one million times more powerful than our conscious mind. Ninety-five percent of brain activity is beyond our conscious awareness. Only five percent of our cognitive activities (decisions, actions, behavior) are aware, whereas the remaining ninety-five percent created in a non-conscious manner. It mirrors the universe; five percent of stars or matter and ninety-five dark matter and energy. It consists of saved or stored information that one applies to a situation, like a large data center or repository which permanently keeps every moment that has ever happened to you. It means that how you grew up is always running behind the scenes in your mind. It affects your conscious thought about everything; traffic, work, relationships, people, spending money, you name it. It influences one's actions and emotions. That's why you sometimes experience fear, anxiety, or depression without wanting to. Those unconscious thoughts are your past.

It's imperative to tap into your subconscious mind's destructive thoughts and change it with your conscious mind. Working on accepting whatever issues reside in you is how you rewire your brain. It begins with self-forgiveness. Forgiving will set you free and allow you to erase things in your past that affect your life. Eliminate living in the past and learn the lessons, so you do not get stuck in life, you keep growing. By doing this, you will be allowing yourself out of the emotional jail, and you won't be the thought prisoner anymore. You won't be sitting around wondering whether you did something wrong or pondering why something did not work out. You accepted it, forgave yourself and all involved; even things you know were wrong. It's your life, not anyone else's; you can choose to be upset or happy. Sometimes the best thing to do from a bad experience is to just let it go.

Ultimately, changing your subconscious mind should you have had painful events or endure emotions from the past that will calm your life. And should you open to the universe, love to your heart. You are the tree, the internal lessons learned are the underground roots, the deeper you go within, the more significant the growth on the outside. Sit back and allow the universe to work for you. This one change will get you out of the darkness. There is light at the end of the tunnel, rewire yourself, everybody can, however, there is only one person who can do that for you, that's you! Are you thinking yet?

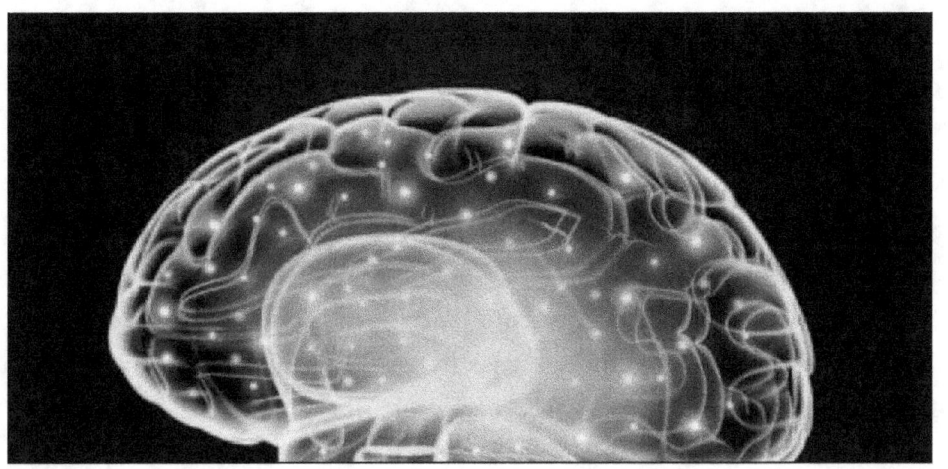

How your Brain is Wired

"The hand that rocks the cradle is the hand that rules the world."
– Anonymous

Scientists say your brain is wired by the time you turn six to eight years old. The subconscious part of our brain and the way we think when we grow older is developed by the people who surround us as a kid. Much like they say a kid's mind is a sponge, watch your language, it's the same for behavior. The relationship we have with our parents and siblings will mold us. This series of events within our subconscious mind is the challenge most will face in life. However, we have the power to release any energy and reshape our subconscious mind.

When you slow down and take the time to look within yourself in your life, a pattern will form. You will find you have participated in the same type of relationships your whole life. Once you have recognized this pattern, a weird thing happens about how you thought about them and your behaviors. You will not have realized your childhood has been churning away behind the scenes in your subconscious mind forever. You find you were oblivious to the pattern. However, once you recognize the model, a new light is cast upon you, and you can change the design. That light allows you to grow and become whole, one with your soul and to follow the love of your soul.

Your brain is wired for the love the universe has given you. When we do not think with love, we are open to wrong thoughts, which physically damages your brain. With proper thinking, you can rewire your mind to build healthy replacement thoughts and new brain pathways. The synapses in your brain (the junction between two nerve cells, consisting of a gap across which impulses pass by diffusion of a neurotransmitter) connect to your thoughts. Your every single thought impacts the seventy-five to one-hundred trillion cells in your body. Good ideas build more positive synapse bridges as your brain controls your entire body, and it accomplishes the will of your soul. Whatever you think, builds more of these bridges and takes you down that path of life.

Your soul directs the body, which is led by the spirit. Your spirit is the connection to the love of the universe. Your thought life determines most of the power of how you function. You are unique and designed by the all-powerful universe. When your mind prospers, your body and spirit prosper. You have chosen to listen to the voice inside and the love in your soul. When you have a toxic thought or make a mistake, your body's immune system recognizes it the same way it recognizes a virus or physical wound and begins to contain it. When you have fear-based thoughts, you feel fear throughout your physical body. Fear takes control over your entire body. When you find yourself in the fear zone, look to the universe and connect to the infinite love. Fear is the absence of love, and you have the power, through your thoughts, to move from fear to love.

How do I recognize my thought patterns? You begin by analyzing what you think about all the time, address the issues causing you pain, guilt, shame, and fear. You accept and address those emotions, forgive yourself, others, and let them go. You cannot control the events and circumstances of life; sometimes, they result from other people's choices. You can control how you react to the facts and circumstances of life. You're a supernatural child of the universe, always remember that. By moving to a place of forgiveness, you allow yourself to heal. Once you practice this over and over, that thought then moves to your subconscious mind. You will erase the time you spend lamenting the past, and you will not be the prisoner anymore of your thoughts. You will live in the present and become yourself again. You allow yourself to become happy and find new, loving people who create happy memories with you. That will enable you to find inner happiness and a path to your meaning.

Forgiveness is the pillar of internal health and love. Love is natural; anger and fear are learned. By injecting loving actions into every thought and situation, you will see a difference in the outcomes, and people will see a difference in you. You will understand forgiveness frees you. You will realize you are not the person anymore that lives in the past; you learned the lesson. You recognized the source of the hurt and self-healed. Rewiring your brain is a very conscious thought process and may take years; however, learning through mistakes will allow you to stay on the path of enlightenment and change your life.

I was wired differently than most; I have no idea why, however, seemed lucky throughout my early years; maybe it was the Irish side. I would catch the biggest fish, harvest the largest buck, but that all started to change when I lost my connection with the universe. I let my egoic mind run my life. I had no idea this was even happening, and probably a lot of you do not either. So, when my brother passed away, I got divorced, my job(s) sucked because I did, my thoughts affected my energy around all living things. I changed, I wasn't myself anymore, and I was highly destructive to myself. I had changed through evil thoughts about myself, life, and people. Not until I faced self-induced struggles, bad connections, and people connected to the universe that showed another way of thinking, did I understand. I changed myself back through positive, loving internal thoughts and actions. I realized all my issues were created by me, my thoughts, not others. You can do the same. When you use your mind, you can do anything in life.

Understanding how you are wired is an excellent first step why you think the way you do. Are you hurt inside? A victim? Fearful of your future? Are you scared of love? Dig in and uncover why. You will discover it has something to do with your thoughts. Move out of that darkness and into the light of love. Understanding the subconscious thoughts in your mind takes time, do not rush it. Then begin by removing the negative thoughts when they occur by telling yourself that is not how you think anymore. Rewire your brain to see the truth about yourself and your life. Then manifest what you seek with your mind and believe.

Begin by enjoying every minute of your life; it will be over before you know it. Speak with older adults at a nursing home; their greatest regret is wasting time thinking about things that upset them. Mainly their guilty past, their fearful future, or how someone hurt them. You must practice letting things go as anger will destroy you. Anger is what covers hurt emotions and fear. Next time you are angry, trace the origin to the root; shame, fear, hurt, embarrassment, disappointment, or impatience? Take a moment before you express anger to determine what you want to accomplish. Living with emotions will only destroy you. Start the conversation with yourself that everything that happens to you is not personal and address those emotions causing you anger and conquer them. No matter what is going on in your life, realize you are not dead, how blessed you are, and the little things don't matter.

Achieving a state free of negative emotions is challenging; however, the adverse is it will only bring you misery and disease. There are new ideas and studies out there that claim you attract whatever you give thought energy towards. They claim our thoughts and the things we harbor in our hearts, such as anger, fear, envy, jealousy, cause our genes to reproduce those dark thoughts into dark cells. This manifests into more significant internal energy clusters and create different forms of cancers. They are groundbreaking and said to influence you and even how your offspring think and grow mentally and physically. These genes are passed on from generation to generation. Be the change and change that pattern by living in the present and enjoy your life, every day.

We should all channel our energy and thoughts to our lives and what we want it to be. It's not a present thought to think this way. And I am not talking about only thinking only about yourself. Rewiring your brain is tough stuff and takes practice. When you recognize your thoughts and words as the most potent things we own, you realize we are energetic beings. Everything is energy, and everything has a cause and an effect. You become your thoughts. You bring everything to you with your ideas. Although your soul is the purest form and guides you in life, your thoughts attract what you seek.

I never said it would quickly happen, or happiness would suddenly overtake you. Give yourself some time. This change may take a year or five years. Everything worthwhile in life takes time and commitment. No pain, no gain. Understand you have this one current life, live it to the fullest, and attract what you seek. When you think this way you become balanced, you balance the love and fear and find joy on the inside. Rewire your brain to focus on channeling your energy to you, your dreams, and what you manifest your life to be. Rewire your brain to see the beauty of yourself and the whole world. Forget the past; you cannot go back. Rewire your mind to see the beauty of the universe. By letting go of negative thoughts, learning your lessons, and having empathy for all living creatures, you rewire your mind to allow the abundance of the gifts of the universe to bring you joy. You understand that life is a blessing and meant to experience pleasure.

THE LITTLE VOICE INSIDE

"There's a voice inside you that tells you what you should do."
– Alan Rickman

Do you ever have a gut feeling? Had an intuition? Do you ever wonder whether you should stay away from someone or someplace? End a relationship? Have you ever been to the grocery store, not hungry, and some thought says get that? You then ponder those thoughts and say, I do not want to spend the money, or I already have some at home. You get home or a day or two later, you look for that item, and it's empty, almost empty or not there at all and you go, damn, why didn't I listen to that little voice inside me? I have. We all face this is a never-ending series of choices. What is that voice? Let's see.

Trusting yourself and your inner voice is a conscious decision. The sound is inside everyone, whether you believe it or not. You must decide to listen and connect. That little voice inside you is the guardian angel that protects you and guides you. In some circles, it's called a divine spirit, the holy spirit, or our soul's love. Call it what you like, however we all that voice of intuition inside us. It's your second brain attempting to guide you to do something to help you down your path. That voice will lead you to something to find on your way when you didn't even know you needed it. I'm not saying to jump off a bridge here; I am saying to follow that voice. Your soul is always leading you, guiding you, encouraging you, and loving you. It's your destiny and purpose inside you. Decipher the real voice inside, listen to your soul, and follow it.

We all search for areas in our lives where we need to change and grow. When we do this, a robust process moves into motion, which ultimately helps us become better beings. The little voice works within us, guiding us to put into action what we learn. It's our gut intuition we trust—a clear understanding without experiencing fear. Your gut intuition exists from your past experiences. When we understand we are living souls that flesh surrounds and your intuition is your soul's consciousness, we see and act differently. We do not allow our minds always to lead. When guided by our soul's knowledge, we are led to a higher place and do the right thing.

The little voice can be understood when we are paying attention to the inner self. All of life's battles begin in the mind. When we always follow the brain, we lose touch with what the heart is telling us. Although we are unable to hear the struggle inside physically, we listen to it in our heads. When we look, we receive instructions to enhance our lives in some manner. The inner voice leads the spirit with the love of the universe. We are being driven by our soul to set in motion something that will favor us on our path.

We hear our inner voice daily; some may seem insignificant. However, the instructions are substantial learning lessons. The little voice works within us, subtle and straightforward. When you follow that voice, you will be given directions to life goals in a huge way. You must be ready to hear the little voice at work and act on it. Doing so is exercising the guidance of our soul. For example, did I stand up for myself today when someone treated me wrongly? Did I speak from the heart? I had a great idea, and the voice said to write it down, and the ego said, I'll remember, and you forgot? You must listen to that inner voice. Only then can you grow and decipher the messages. Attune yourself to the quiet little voice that works in your mind that is leading you to do what is right. A soft voice, so pay attention or you will miss it. Listen and let that voice guide you to the principles of the universe; to the love, the kindness, the charity, the humility, patience, and forgiveness. Act on those actions when the voice speaks. It may save your life one day. Listen when it speaks to you.

My parents and I were headed back to San Antonio, Texas, from Dallas, Texas, one day in the 1990s, visiting my brother. We were behind this rise in the road, and there was an accident ahead. There was heavy traffic and we at a standstill. Behind us, an eighteen-wheeler rolled over the top of a rise in the road about seventy-five miles an hour. My dad was driving, and I saw the fear in his face in the rear-view mirror, and he said, "oh shit." He could have pulled to the left or stayed put. He stayed put. The big rig slid past us to the left on the shoulder and flew by with grass and dirt flying everywhere. I am sure we all would have died. He said, "I'm glad I didn't move left; something inside me said to stay still." The voice had saved us.

The little voice is a mechanism we all want to fight in our lives. It's a natural response to our subconscious mind. A path laid out from the universe. The voice tells you when to get out of a bad situation. The voice also guides you to your happiness. Take the advice! We have all been there. The voice steers you in the right direction. Do not dismiss it. It will figure something out you have been thinking about for a time. Ask the voice for answers when you become still on the inside. It will show how beautiful our precious life is. Your soul is the essence of you, the purest thing you own and guiding you. Listen to and use that inner voice!!!

LETTING GO

"The truth is unless you let go, unless you forgive yourself, unless you forgive the situation, unless you realize that the situation is over, you cannot move forward."
– Steve Maraboli

Everything in the universe has a process of letting go and allowing for growth. The universe will always make you let go of something before it enables you to take hold of something. When we travel our path of growth, we must let go of something or someone to continue our journey. We are naturally growing, evolving, and building our lives. We are born to develop our vibration to a higher level to achieve our purpose. When we allow our ego to tell us not to let go, we experience the thoughts that our life is working against us. When we attempt to hang on to our past, a bad relationship, or an unfulfilling job, we only delay the growth process. We end up upset and weigh ourselves down. Then our energy levels suffer. When we learn to release the bad and embrace the good, the abundance of growth takes place. Let's explore this.

Letting go in life is something you need to comprehend to understand what is behind it entirely. When we learn the process, we find out life isn't working against us, it's working with us. Our soul knows how to strengthen our vibration; it's what the universe is all about. It's the divine plan for us. It's about trusting and having faith in the process that allows us to obtain it. We end up growing spiritually or closer to ourselves through the process. When releasing who or what that is no longer bringing growth or serving our highest good, we release the negative energy. We realize the who and what has been blocking the way to our growth with our wasted energy. By having the courage to release the who or what, we begin the process of personal growth.

We are our best teachers when it comes to our personal growth on all levels. The answers reside inside all of us. The little voice has been telling us for a long time. However, we must master the lesson of letting go of what no longer serves us. Holding on to the past, guilt, shame, or people is an excuse for some type of pain inside. It's an excuse for our behavior. It's not my fault; it's their fault. Ever say that in your mind? Very confusing and challenging. Holding on is a coping mechanism to cover the trapped emotions in our subconscious mind and our soul's pain. However, we must enisle the source of the pain to begin the process.

Many situations we find ourselves in, we put our self there whether we believe that or not with our thoughts. When we accept that and quit the blame game of others, we look within for the path that got us there. Sometimes the way is foolish, and other times our spirit leads us to or away from people or situations. When we do understand how we got into a bad situation, attempt to control your thoughts to stay away from anger, attempt not to take offense, or beat yourself up when things do not turn out as we want. Instead, reward yourself when they are right. Lessons are very tough sometimes and letting go of something your ego wants is even harder.

When we sit back and comprehend, we allow ourselves to release the bad and embrace the good. When we open our minds and embrace steps to heal, we give ourselves a chance to experience growth in our lives and happiness in our hearts. Fear of the unknown is a big reason we do not want to let go. The fear of being alone, finding someone else, or something to replace what we let go. Anxiety, worry, and fear. When we hold on to people that no longer bring some form of growth in our lives, we become stuck, and our energy suffers. Then we look for external outlets, buying things, going out somewhere with someone for the wrong reasons, or taking substances to fill that hole. The more hurt, the more we look to this for our happiness. However, by learning how to let go, you will find this is a growth mechanism in life to maintain inner happiness.

Letting go of things that matter to us is difficult. We have all been hurt or perceived hurt in some form or fashion by someone in our lives. When we dwell on the negative side of anything, we get stuck in life. We then suffer through a period of hurt. We can lose ourselves and miss the boat of life. The converse of acceptance is the truth. When you address the situation with an open mind that is paying attention, you learn why you want to let go in the first place. You learn about self-love, happiness, and what matters in life. The journey is to find joy and happiness on the inside. You must let go to grow as everything has a season. Life and relationships have a season, never settle for unhappiness.

Here are a few steps to practice letting go.

Find the time to quiet your mind from all the distractions of the world. Turn off the television, get off your computer, and hide the smartphone. Find the stillness in your life and breathe. Just get comfortable somewhere and think with your eyes closed and take deep breaths and exhales. Focus on whatever issues are bothering you. Then ask, does this person or thing figure into my life's goals, beliefs, and values? Do they bring me some form of growth in life or pain? Should you remain still and clear your mind, the answers will come over time. Then manifest the results in your mind or write them down. Then act on those revelations. This process begins to release the lower-vibrational energy inside us by letting go of the who or what.

Once you have addressed the issue(s), it's how you think the situation should have played out. Because someone did something you perceived as wrong, remember, the other person may not believe they did anything wrong. Not everyone thinks like you. Those are the false expectations. It's like waiting around for an apology that is never going to come, that's inner prison, and you are the prisoner. Break out of the inner prison, let it go and forgive. The power to forgive and letting go releases us from the prison of pain, hurt, or perceived mistreatment. It brings back self-empowerment. It takes the ability to look within to do this and self-love. You can do this! The reward is the freedom to use your energy to create what gives your life happiness and the ability to attract your dreams.

Using thought to move past anything is one thing, living it is another. That's the tough part. You will find over time that letting go of things will open a brand-new life for you. The comforts of releasing the pain and then seeing all the rewards and abundance are priceless. The growth can take some time, so be flexible and allow the path to open. An increase in life takes courage, faith, and strength. And, every relationship has taught you something about yourself. Incorporate the lessons you learned into your life and use it. You are blessed to be alive. Life is a lot tougher out there for some. Release hurtful things in your life that bring you down; they are only blocking the way.

Most of us take life for granted; we expect to wake up the next morning. Life is a blessing and a beautiful thing, not a hassle. We make it trouble with our negative thoughts and actions. When we remove all the non-growth mechanisms in our lives, it brings about a new outlook, and we become grateful for what we have. When we learn that letting go of hurtful events is not about others, it's about ourselves. When we live in a state of love, forgiving, and choose love to solve our issues with ourselves and others, no matter what has happened. We learn to let go and change the tire. When we decide not to forgive, we are imprisoning all involved. Practicing forgiveness of self and others creates freedom for everyone involved. You will realize that being offended is not about the person who hurt you; it's about yourself. You may as well let it go quickly because you eventually will, save yourself all that drama and churn.

When things happen to you that seem wrong or unfair, step back and figure how you got there. Only you can manage your feelings, do not permit others; you will lose control of yourself. With your ideas, become the eagle that flies above the storm clouds of drama and anger. Be the eagle that soars above the despair one can put themselves in. Stay high as being low only makes you doubt your greatness. Doubt and fear are evil; happiness and love are the essences of life on the inside. Become happy and don't allow the drama of the day or someone else to control their emotions. Let go, like OB1 told Luke to use the force when he blew up the Death Star, use the force of love and forgiveness inside you. Be the hero to yourself, not the prisoner, and let go of all the things that hold you back.

We should never judge or not accept a person for whom he or she is. It's not healthy to endure any friendship or relationship that doesn't make us better. Surround yourself with people who make you better and that care for you. Be in the company of people who make you proud they are in your life. Do not latch on to someone who will gamble with your heart or mind because they know you are too attached. End friendships or relationships that are damaging, making you unhappy or miserable. Find people that treat you as whole and worthy, not a one-sided relationship. Never allow anyone to make you feel needy for wanting their love, care, and support; find people who want the same things. You can trust and believes in yourself and your dreams. Someone that makes you sense you are somebody. Someone who makes you comfortable being who you are, as you are. Release people in your life that do not make you feel this way. Be the person, no matter how difficult and lonely it may be, to let go of damaging people. You will become much happier, and you will attract growth in the areas you are manifesting for yourself.

Letting go is about the self. It's about understanding the person and opening to the understanding of what patience, kindness, tolerance, and empathy are. We then can stop the blame game of others and create a new way for ourselves, families, and others we love. We accept what is right in our face. We come to a point in life to live from a position of greater appreciation, intention, and purpose because we are free from the inner struggle. We then ask ourselves why people act the way they do before we rush to judgment of them. That leads us to the understanding of why we operate the way we do. It's a moment of clarity. We then understand that happiness and joy are the duty of the self, and when someone is taking that from us, we need to release something or someone. When we accept that we must release damaging things in our lives, we learn that letting go changes everything and is the door to a new growth transition.

One day I was at work, and they had this grand opening for a new building remodel. You received this card and traveled around different product groups who would stamp the map to win prizes. The main prize was a 2-in-1 laptop. So, I went around, had my card filled out, signed my name, and threw it in a big glass bowl. As I threw it in, I said to myself, I am going to win something. That day we had a visitor from out of town who does our financing. He took my whole team to lunch. When I returned, I had all kinds of people, about twenty, tell me, "That was an expensive lunch," "where have you been," did know they called your name for the grand prize." I mean it was everywhere, the bathroom, hallways and at my desk. You had to be present to win the prizes. I was like, "wow." A girl that sits next to me said, "boy that sucks that you didn't win that laptop," and about four other people chimed in. I stood up and said in a polite, calm voice, "I refuse to be the prisoner, that was fate, someone else needed that laptop way more than me and the universe made sure that happened." They were all shocked, they wanted me to be upset and mad, and some even said that. I said, I never owned it, so I am letting it go, and you should too—the looks I received. However, should you not release these things in life, it will destroy you.

Letting go of something or someone is robust and may linger in your thoughts for some time, it's natural. However, should you allow this to continue to bother you, it will destroy you. Have you ever seen angry people in the world? Not all as we all have a bad day; however, the clear majority have never learned to let go. The negative energy must go somewhere. It will cause some form of internal illness, cancer, and destroy your vibration. Many books describe negative inner emotions that cause disease; read them. They are fascinating and insightful. Let whatever is damaging you go. You will experience what self-love is all about, loving yourself over a laptop, a bad relationship, a disloyal friend, betrayal, or some hardship you have faced. It will only make you stronger and lead to growth. There is no reason to live in anger with anything or anyone. Control what you can control. Only you can manage your thoughts and emotions. Do your best in all situations. Love all the time, and do not allow anyone or anything to steal your love. Practicing letting go of negatives in your life will open the growth and abundance of the universe. So, you know, not everyone is going to love and like you. Why live with that expectation? Find the people who do, and you will be much happier. Let all the drama in your life that your ego creates go! Your happiness and dreams are waiting for you when you do.

"I believe that everything happens for a reason. People change so that you can learn to let go; things go wrong so that you appreciate them when they're right, sometimes good things fall apart so better things can fall together."
– Marilyn Monroe

Everything has a Season

"Every new season of your life will be an opportunity for you to learn and grow. Don't celebrate the good without celebrating the bad because they both work together to prepare you for the next season of your life."
– Theresa Lewis

Do you ever wonder when winter is going to end, or summer to begin? When it will be spring with the perfect weather? When the flowers will bloom, and the leaves return to the trees? When the new animal offspring will be born or hatch? Why our loved ones died? Everything has a season. Everything in the universe has a season. Planets exist for a while and then bang; some other object hits it, and it's gone. All types of stars, plants, animals, and weather have a season. And so, do our relationships, jobs, cars, everything has a season. Life has a season. Everything we participate in our lives has a season and will end. Learn to recognize the present moment in every season, so you do not miss the opportunity to create lasting memories with the ones you love. It's our spirit leading us through every season, creating memories and every open or closed door of our relationships. All seasons will have a beginning and an end.

Do you ever wonder what happened to that friend from elementary school, an old friend, or a neighbor? That was a season. Your spirit, whether you believe this or not, guides you to some form of outcome. No matter what has happened between you and someone else in the past, it happened just how it was supposed to be the person you are today and learn something. That is why you should not live in the former state of mind or your perceived mistakes. Mistakes are your spirit leading you to new accomplishments, people, and your dreams. Mistakes lead you into a season. When you dwell on the past and in your mistakes, you and your life will suffer. You will become stuck at a place in time and miss the messages for your ultimate path.

We are living in the age of Aquarius, the age of enlightenment. Humans have been building up to this age since the beginning of time. We all have an astrological blueprint, and so does our planet. The age of Aquarius is a time and connection to the universe that has exponential growth in the evolution of knowledge and technology for humankind. Do some research should you want to dive further deep. Look around the next time you go anywhere and see all the new technology in our lives. All of it, everything has a meaning; I mean everything. Look past the obvious; you will learn something. However, many of us are lost in the world of smartphones, television, streaming, video games, and the flesh. We are not paying attention to the inside of us, only the external. When we do not follow the spirit, we miss the many messages that surround us. Then when something we perceive as wrong happens to us in this external world, we can become stuck in life. We only see the bad and not the good. Sometimes, some of us never sit back, turn the page, and decipher the overall outcome. We allow the result to become us and our future. That is the dark side of life, the light is when you let life flow, relax and embrace whatever happens. That is the light of your spirit leading you. That is how you learn the lessons of the soul.

Your failures are preparing you. All our faults are preparing us to learn, correct and love our self more. People usually take failure the other way and live in despair about it. We see ourselves in a dark mode and then turn to other vices to mask the hurt. We give up on an idea or their dreams. We settle in the dark. Then we reach a low point and can only move in one direction, up and into the light or we get stuck in the despair. The dark of despair is where fear and the ego want to keep you. However, when we are led out of that darkness, the spirit is guiding us to find the strength inside to fix ourselves, gain the confidence and love our self. Everybody makes mistakes, nobody is perfect. We all make mistakes, trust me, I have made unknown countless mistakes with people. Only we can cancel our mistakes or our destinies, we must forgive and believe in our self. It's not how others see you, it's how we see ourselves that gets us through the season. We must listen to the spirit to guide us out of the darkness we can get ourselves in.

The universe chooses you to live at this moment in history to teach and learn lessons. Sometimes you must go through a bad season, the dark, to get to the light. It's like being lost in the forest, you have no idea where you are at, where you are going and whether you will even survive. We do the same with our lives. We go through many of life's challenges-not paying attention and through things we don't understand. We are led into these situations for a reason and sometimes we have no idea how we got there. That is the spirit guiding you to learn a lesson and to the light. Everyone is led out into the desert to learn something about themselves and make themselves better. When this does happen, do right thing as much as possible, let go and surrender to the outcome. A new opportunity will present itself to end the season. Then let the season go and become the person you want to be. Your spirit is leading you through this dark season to your purpose. Be humble and patient as the universe will use your failures to promote you to do something amazing in your life.

Sometimes you did your best, and it didn't work out. That person you loved, the job, friends, it's a bad season. Control what you can control. Then attempt to let go of your past, a terrible manager, a person who stole from you, and not become stuck in a season. We move through so many seasons in our lives that we cannot afford to live in only one. When we do get stuck, we will miss the opportunities that present themselves. We blame the world for our problems. We must come to an understanding that all issues and problems are the responsibility of the self. They are presented to learn something. By forgiving yourself, forgiving others, are kind, and loving, the lousy season will end.

Everything has a season. Your life is like a long baseball or football season. Think about all the time, practice, meetings, games and possibly playoffs that goes into those seasons. Like your life, you have all these phases. Should you get stuck somewhere along the way, you can never become who the universe wants you to be. Only you can control your thoughts, emotions and love. Understand the phase of the season you are in. Then, be on time, practice everything, play hard, accept where you are at and excel once you get the opportunity. Understanding that a season will end allows you to live in the present moment and not allow other thoughts to cloud the moment. Seasons are meant to begin and end. They are intended to teach how to love, let go and forgive.

Seasons and your spirit are guiding you to your purpose. Only by understanding that everything will end one day, allows you to be the best in the present moment. It enables you to let go of little things, open about your emotional past, end or grow relationships, end the practice of complaining about meaningless things, bring gratitude to the surface of everything and a sense of joy to be alive. Your season will end one day; however, the many seasons you will pass through during your lifetime will determine whether you are happy or angry at the end. Do you best in all situations, take the high road, use love for all issues and understand that everything has a season. There is a reason why some are remembered after they pass away, they left a legacy and let go of all the wrong seasons. They embraced the moment and did not allow an opportunity to pass in any season. Seasons come, and they go, it's how you grow from them that will determine where you move through life. Live in the season, live life like you're on vacation and let your spirit guide you. You may not understand the season, that's your eyes, sense it in your soul and you will make it through any season.

A buddy of mine is sixty-seven years old, rides his bike every day, pretty in-shape, 6'1", friendly guy with grey hair. He played in the NFL (National Football League) as a receiver. He started as a kid, played through middle school, high school, and attended a Big-8 Conference university on a football scholarship. After he graduated, he was drafted by the San Diego Chargers. After he left that organization, he played for a while in the USFL (United States Football League) in San Antonio, Texas. During a game, he tore a nerve in his leg, and it was over. All that hard work for all those years was over in an instance. The season was over for him, and the season of his life in football was over. He let it all go and embraced the accomplishment. He is now a financial advisor and spends his time playing golf. I think he made it through that season.

Everything has a season in your life. It's essential to understand and to move on from every season and not get stuck there. That is where the growth is, that is where the abundance lies and that is where you find your purpose, conquering, understanding and moving through every season in your life. You do this by forgiving yourself, forgiving others and loving yourself. You can walk through any season in life, you must believe in yourself and remain optimistic about your future.

Are you in a good or bad season now?

Well, hopefully you understand to follow your spirit to something great. All seasons will end, manifest what you want the outcome to be and you will conquer any season. Seasons are meant for you to learn about and love yourself. Embrace what you learn from every season, not the season itself. I believe you can conquer any season in your life. Stay on the path your spirit guides you to, it's showing you your future and demonstrating how to grow from every season. Remember, you must let go to grow and it's not what you want, it's how much pain you want to go through to achieve what you want. Keep growing and learn from every season. I believe in you, do you?

THE PATH

*"No one saves us but ourselves. No one can, and no one may.
We ourselves must walk the path."*
– Buddha

What is this "The Path"? We all go through life and when we think we have it figured out, BOOM, sometimes, the exact opposite. Why do we do this? Why do we think we know so much? A path will lead you somewhere, they all do. A circle never gets you anywhere, you go around and around. We walk around and never take the time to stop and think whether we are living in a circular rut. Desires of all kinds are a circular path. They lead you to the same place. We keep coming back again and again to the same desires. That is why some of us never find joy as desires are unquenchable. No one ever gets anywhere chasing them and contentment is impossible. In the end, one will waste their whole life chasing unattainable desires that will never happen, or should they, will not meet their expectations. That is why the aim to happiness in life is the love of self, and truth, then one will not be content with anything else. It's a real blessing as only by passing through that journey of self-love can one find the ultimate contentment. Let's explore this.

We are all on a journey or a path in life. The quest for truth. All truths, especially the truth about ourselves and the ability to accept it. To embrace the truth no matter what has happened to us. That is what builds our character. Those who search for the truth must be committed and ready for this change. When they do, they find the truth will come looking for them. Some of us recognize this as we continue to grow and some of us are blind to it. Most people never search for the truth and never let go of most things, it's human. They never release some beliefs they have created within themselves. Have you ever stretched the truth about a story you told? The truth path leads you somewhere. When you use the truth to get you there, the truth will always set you free.

We all have a path set out for us before we are even born, imagine that. However, we have free will and an ego that leads us off our path sometimes. The trail is made up of many experiences that flow through our mind, body and soul. Like the Ant and the Grasshopper story, prepare for your life's path. We all come across a new opportunity or a karmic event and an original path is born. The new job, the new love, the new baby, a new way. A lesson to conquer success, fear, love and life. A test of your faith to consciously use your mind and inner strength to succeed. Life is a test; you must believe in yourself to pass it. The tough breaks only teach you and raise you up, not pull you down. No pain, no gain, especially for the soul.

Remaining on your path in life is very important. You must become aware that you are on one. Your path leads you somewhere, it's your destiny. It's leading you to your purpose. You may have the little voice inside you that says, I want to be a doctor, I want to be an engineer, or I want to be a teacher. That's part of your path, so listen to that voice guiding you. You must realize it and work for it should you want to accomplish it. Follow your passion, not the money. You will be way for successful. In the end, it's not about what you want, it's about how much pain you want to go through to get it.

Many people live in insanity, meaning doing the same things repeatedly expecting a different result. They are spinning their wheels, going in a circle. They keep moving in the same direction. They are chasing money and their desires repeatedly. It's when you become aware and wake up to the distraction, the truth of your life will present itself. Give yourself the space and time to understand your path and journey. When you do, the good things in life will come your way. Visualize what you want to do with your life and get out of whatever rut you may be in, like a bad friendship, an unhealthy relationship or scheduling your whole life around watching something on TV. Then manifest your dreams in your heart and work for them. Create a location in your home with pictures of the things you want in your life and then concentrate your energy to them daily. People who visualize their dreams, believe in them and speak the power into the universe will achieve them. Never give up on your dreams or on people, they will both pleasantly surprise you.

I wanted to be a veterinarian when I was a kid. Even though I hunt and fish, I love animals. I love everything remember. And so, should you. I think I did because I knew this girl, I was very attracted to whose father was a veterinarian. I never pursued it and I'm not upset about it as I started thinking about working with all those animals and having to deal with the bad ones. After all that wasn't my path. I graduated with a Bachelor's Degree in Business Administration. I was good at talking with people, so I gravitated to sales. Shocker. Well, that was my path. What I am telling you here is that we all end up somewhere in life our way. We must realize and visualize what we want to become along the path and put the wheels into motion.

Most people get stuck in the 3D world and chase the wrong things. I did for a very long time, what horse poo. You will stumble off course when you only trust your own "sense of direction" your emotions, desires, or personal version of everything. When you only pursue what's looks right instead of the knowledge you receive from the universe. You will keep asking yourself, "what did I do wrong?" When you chase the right things, it will all come to fruition. Wait for it as this does not happen overnight, and do not get in a hurry. Good things come to those who wait. Stay seated and allow the universe to work for you. Something will open for you when you stay positive.

You start out by believing in yourself. Nobody is going to believe in you unless you believe in yourself. Then you surround yourself with the people who build you up, are loving, and are thriving. Then start to release people and jobs that cause you drama or question your spirit. Leave these situations no matter how much it hurts. The universe will reward you with a better job and loving people. Should you still be upset where you land at, change surroundings to get you back on the right track. Continue until you find peace on the inside. Nobody is going to do this for you.

By educating yourself to the world around you and what precisely you want to do, and you work hard, you do the research, you will find your path. Happiness comes from inside you, not the external world. It's like the fortune cookie I received when I was down and out one day that stated, "when you are happy, you are successful." It's about opening all the possibilities in your mind and empowering yourself to move forward, through the fear and to rewire your brain with the confidence to do so. It's about focusing on "your path" and changing your life forever by acting on your thoughts and putting them into action. It's about channeling your energy to your life and what you manifest your life to be. That is the path to fulfillment and happiness in life.

We are all bombarded by information these days about what others think our path should be. It's everywhere. Everyone should go to college for example. I disagree. Some people do not want that, they want to be electricians, welders, plumbers, auto mechanics or in the building trades. I say let them. I say bring this training back into the high schools. These young people can learn a trade and work for someone for five to ten years and then open their own businesses. Then they can take care of their families, not pay off some student loan the rest of their life. I rambled, what I am explaining is a path to happiness. When we are successful in our life, whether its love, our job or our family, or all of them, we bring joy to ourselves. That in turn brings out the joy in the people we love and care for. That makes everyone enjoy living more. It allows you to see more clearly what life is about. It will enable you to see your future and be excited about it. Stay on your path of happiness!

The path is sometimes very unclear, mine was. I was way off, and people get off their path, and they do not even know it. They watch their smartphone all day and get caught up in everybody else's drama. They end up missing the world and the people around them. They miss that special someone they have been seeking; maybe they were at the same place; perhaps they had them in their life and played games; however, they were too interested in themselves. Or too busy worrying about other's lives on social media to realize it. Or maybe they are sitting at home playing video games or watching porn. You make a choice here. Sharing your life with others and with the people you love is the essence of life. The universe does not give you the people you want; you are given the people you need to help you, hurt you, leave you, and love you to make you the person you were meant to be.

Life is an inside job. You must love yourself to recognize the pitfalls of today and society. You'll never stay on your path, the one you want to be on unless you pay attention to yourself and your happiness. Working every day using love to connect to all living things will guide you. Learn to use love in all situations, no matter how difficult. Be in the moment when speaking with people and speak from the heart. Cease thinking about other people or other situations when you are in a conversation. Cease attempting to win every conversation by thinking about what you are going to say next. Cease wanting always to be right. You will be missing the gist of it all. You will be missing part of the path.

Getting out of your comfort zone every day is an excellent way to learn something new. Exercise your mind, body, and soul so you can physically and mentally accomplish your path. Once you connect to your soul, your soul will guide you. Clarity will emerge to where your life is headed. Write down your goals, live them, manifest where you want to be in six months. Once you have accomplished your goals, set new ones. Help others on their path by being friends and understand their hardships. Do not allow today's distractions to steer you off the road; stay focused every day. You are the only driver on your path. You are the only one that knows where you are going. Get there in style, not unhappiness. It's up to you, believe in yourself. I believe in you!

THE ENERGY

*"If you want to find the secrets of the universe,
think in terms of energy, frequency, and vibration."*
– Nikola Tesla

You know that family member, friend, co-worker, or someone who always has issues? They always find something or someone to complain about, no matter where they go. The place is too cold; the food was not that good; this person at work said or did something. I never knew there were so many people out in the world like this. Some people call them a Debbie Downer, a drama queen, or they are just insecure and want everyone to be uncomfortable like them. We detect the negative energy and do not want to be around them. Their negative actions, thoughts, energy, and vibration can bring the whole room down. They drain everyone's enjoyment. Well, those folks do not know how to tap into their vibration and create positive energy. Let's discuss that.

One day I was leaving work, a Friday, and headed to this beautiful place to just chill, eat some healthy appetizers and get a few drinks, imagine that. It was a beautiful day outside, sun shining, clouds blowing by, and birds chirping in the green oak trees. I rolled up with the windows down and the radio up. It was packed. It was like five-fifteen, what the? They had a valet service; however, I am weird about that and always park myself. I rolled around the parking lot three or four times, praying to the parking angel, and nothing opened. I had to send this package, sunglasses I love to be repaired in Florida, and decided to do that and then head over to the usual watering hole in my neighborhood. I took care of the package and found my usual parking spot at this place.

I rolled in, and there was this older man that had been a US Marine in Vietnam, I think, or Korea. I told him, hello, and we chatted for about twenty minutes until he left. There were these other dudes that I knew, and they said hello, how are you? "We're going to have one more and take off," I said, it's five forty-five PM or so, where you headed? "Home," I said, well, let me put on some music, and we'll go from there. I started jamming some 80's, 90's hairband, classic and alternative rock, my favorites, and the place or the energy picked up. More people kept showing up that knew me and would say and hi and all that. About an hour in, I played another set of music, and this guy shows up at the bar. He looks over and sees me and says, "What the hell bro, how have you been?" I wave, and we chat for a bit, he tells the bartender to put a drink on his tab for me. He goes outside, and that was that. Another dude I haven't seen in a while shows up with his girlfriend. They see me and tell the bartender to put a drink for me on their tab. I go over and thank them and chat for a bit, and then they leave. When I turn around, there is this other guy outside that sees me, comes in, and tells the bartender to put a drink on his tab for me. The woman bartender looked at me with this puzzled look like a ghost or something. I know her, and she never looked at me like that before. I chat it up with the guy, play some more music, and make out the air's energy. Everyone is happy and smiling. This goes on with another guy buying me a drink, and another one comes up, hugs me, and says, "You're my favorite." Now all of this has never happened to me before anywhere or at this place, so I start to sit back and think about the universe and love all that stuff. I look over, and the dudes that were leaving early are still there, talking, laughing, and sending cool hand signals. It's about nine-thirty PM now and my cutoff time as I run Saturday mornings, so I pay up, not much, and head for the side door. As I make my way outside, another dude stops me and says, "Hey, I miss hanging with you," hugs me and says, "We should hang sometime." I tell him that I love him, man love here, I love everyone, and he tells me he loves me. I walked out to the truck and questioned myself, what the hell just happened? Was that I hold the door open stuff and drinks come flying through or what? I felt the energy and love, and so did the people around me. Long story, however, I think you understand what "The Energy" is now. You must let go of all those perceived expectations that bring you down and show up somewhere with positive, living in the moment energy; it is limitless what will happen.

When you think positive thoughts and have faith in yourself daily, that action allows the light of love in, and you find balance. You find inner happiness and attract energy.

I was down at the pool on another glorious warm summer day playing water volleyball with eighteen or so cats and a few girls. We played several games and all that. We pick teams by what time you show up. Show up early; you play right away, show up late, and sit a few games. You tie a shirt on the pole for the next game, and we have this rule that should a team win three in a row, they must disband and be picked up by the captains of the top two shirts. We play to fifteen with no rally scoring, tough for us beer league guys to keep track of. That day I was picked up by this; let's say weaker team, which I do not care anymore as I enacted some rules down there with Rule #1 being to have fun no matter what you are doing in life. We played for a while, and we are losing twelve to three or something.

One of our guys has an enormous spike; I start getting pumped, I start saying, "The Energy, The Energy." (The energy is the feeling when you hear your favorite song and want to get out on the dance floor and get down.) This guy on our team starts serving; he plays sand volleyball two-three times a week, so he is good. He continues getting us point after point, and we start chanting, "The Energy, The Energy." The other team starts looking at us with shock and awe. We keep saving plays and winning points. They start yelling over and are getting upset, and we keep staying pumped and saying, "The Energy." I think you get it. We end up winning with one tremendous spike; I think fifteen to thirteen. My team goes wild. The other side stopped and stared with amazement. That is what the energy is all about—connecting all of us together. When you have high energy that is positive and real, and you believe it to be real, it's contagious.

My new neighbor moved in next door with her sixteen or seventeen your old daughter from Arizona. I believe she was from New York originally. She had all these boxes, and one day after the pool, I said, "Should you need some help, let me know." Nice guy stuff. I didn't hear from her; however, she began to knock on my door and leave me notes. I have some dinner, what you are up to tomorrow, things of that nature, I was busy in life and never stopped by. I would wave at her and sometimes talk, should we arrive home from work at the same time. A few times, we spoke when I saw her in the parking lot, deep, and she said something to the effect that I was on a journey. I didn't think about it, I kept living and working out. It was fifteen months later, and around Christmas, I knocked on her door and gave her some soap and candy. She invited me in, and we chatted for a bit. She told me she had written this poetry book, and we discussed it, then I said I was writing this book. She said, where does the book take you? I explained, and she started to cry.

She said, over the last fifteen months, I have seen the highs and lows of your journey, and I am very proud of you. The energy you give off is undeniable, and there is no mistake why I am your neighbor. I am very spiritual, and we have met in a previous life. Huh internally? I said goodbye after a few more minutes to continue working as that was a work from home day. I didn't think much about it. A few days later, I rolled out to see my son at his job as he was flying to Hawaii with his mother for Christmas.

I get to the restaurant and tell the hostess I'm here and I'll wait for him to come over to the bar when he has a minute. I sit there and have a great conversation with a kid as I ate. He talked about his girlfriend and how much he loved her. They had been together for a long time and on and on. He was under thirty, I believe. I said, why haven't you asked her to marry you? Sirens, flashing lights. He said he had no idea. I explained to him love and people and the universe and how it all works. What you are supposed to do with and for the people you love and that love you. He said, "wow," the answer is clear now. "I am going to visit her family this weekend, and I'm going to ask her father for her hand." He said, "Thank you; you changed my life." I told him, "You are welcome, and you changed your own life. Have a great day." My son then came over, and we hung out a bit, gave him his Christmas presents, and told him to have a great trip and that I loved him.

I then rolled out to see a buddy at his mother's house for a Christmas gathering on my way to the ranch. I was sick. I thought maybe I had the flu. Probably should not have done that. I stayed for three hours and got to the ranch around eight PM, built a fire, went to bed, and slept in the next morning. I awoke even worse and called the local hospital and clinics, nothing open. I found a clinic that was open and drove about thirty-five miles to this small town, the only thing open on Christmas Eve, and signed my name on the list. I had taken this Jen Sincero book to refresh on a few things, as I have read it three or four, maybe five times or more. Jen is a phenomenal thinker! They called my name, my real name, and a nurse escorted me to the patient room.

I spoke with the nurse and told her a guy at work was diagnosed with the flu as I explained my symptoms. She said okay and left. She came back in and swabbed my nose for the flu and said the doctor would be in after. I waited, anxiously, and in came the doctor. A beautiful woman in a white coat; wearing cowboy boots. I said, "Those sure are some nice boots." She said I'm from Wisconsin, and my husband works in San Antonio (Texas), and when we moved, I said I am wearing cowboy boots to work. I said, "bless you; that's awesome." We chatted about life, and she said no flu. She told me there were seven or eight cases of the flu already that day. She spotted the book I brought and asked, "Is that good?" I told her, "it changed my way of thinking about life and changed my life." She said, wow. We talked about life at that moment, and I mentioned I was writing a book, and she smiled. She took a picture of the book I had on the patient table with her phone and said, I want to do some blood work to verify this is not a virus, are you okay with a steroid shot? I said you bet. The nurse came in, gave me the shot, took the blood, and said the doctor would be back when she is available. Ten minutes go by, and she comes back in and says I bought the book on Amazon for ten bucks, I'll be back in two minutes. She comes back in with the results and says, no virus, antibiotics for you. We continue our chat about a few other things, my idea of the book and life, and she says, you have a large energy field around you, and we have met in a previous life. So, this time, I was taken back a bit more. Here I was in this tiny Texas town on Christmas Eve, thinking I'm sick as hell, and all I notice is this energy. She said let me know when the book is published so I can buy one. Your medicine will be ready when you get back to town. I said, "Thank you for everything." I was checking out, and the girl behind the desk asked, "Hey, what is that book in your hand?" I showed her, and she said her friend gave her the book two days ago. The woman doctor who treated me was standing about twenty feet away, heard us speaking, and said, "We are all going to change our lives together." And that was it. Amazing. My understanding of the universe overtook me. It verified that all the thoughts about my vibration that have been flooding my consciousness were real. I became a true believer. The universe, the energy, and the wave I felt from that place. I left to get my medicine on my way to the ranch and thought about it. The energy!

I tell you that you have "The Energy" inside of you, we all do, and it surrounds us. When we let ourselves down with our thoughts, our energy dissipates. When we project our negative thoughts to others, it brings others down. Elevate your thoughts about yourself and quit doubting yourself. Get what you want in life and do it. Nobody is going to do it for you. Allowing ourselves to elevate our thoughts to a positive outcome in life and to believe in ourselves is when the energy increases. Believe in yourself and see your future. Forgive others and yourself. Stay on your path by helping others. That attracts what you are seeking and builds the energy to connect you to the universe. The power will change your life when you tap in, share it with others, and fully believe in it. Pay attention to the energy, and let it guide your soul. Endless possibilities and experiences await you. Tap in, spread it, and you will allow yourself to have experiences you only dreamed of. Be the energy, and the energy will be you.

Illustration by Philipp Schneider : balancedaction.me

FEAR

*"It is not death that a man should fear,
but he should fear never beginning to live."*
– Marcus Aurelius

Oh boy, this is a big one today, and have I been very guilty of this throughout my life. Fear surrounds us everywhere, television, the internet, politics, and in our lives. Anxiety, worry, and fear! Fear is an emotion of something in the future that's not even real. I am afraid to lose my wife, my husband, my job, my money, my house, my mind, and my life. Immigration will destroy us; climate change will destroy us, nuclear war will kill us, and an election will destroy us. I'm afraid to die. Why? Why are we fearful of everything? Some of us aren't; however, a clear majority of people are. Why would you want to live your life afraid to die or all the things mentioned above? Why do we fear so much today?

As humans, we have two emotions, love, and fear. Every emotion spawn from one or the other. Anger is fear under pressure; anxiety is fearing confidence, and only love is the absence of fear. You must balance them out to achieve happiness. Living in a fearful trance will overshadow the truths of life. You will forget about the love of your friends and family, the beauty of the natural world, and everything that is good. You will expect trouble all the time and never live in the present moment. Fear destroys you and your dreams; however, it will create personal growth beyond your goals when you conquer it. Let's dive in and see where we land on this one.

FEAR – False Evidence Appearing Real. What a waste of time and negative energy. What a destructive emotion. Fear is the absence of faith and love. Anger, hate, insecurity is all a type of fear that is under pressure or even worse, made up in our minds. You fear what you do not know. Your soul does not have fear; your brain does. Fear is one emotion that takes much thought to overcome as you must shed the light of love and courage on it. Changing your subconscious mind with conscious thought to remove fear is like changing a tire without a tire iron. It's very tough. However, it can be accomplished with determination and practice.

Understanding why you are afraid of something and challenging yourself to overcome is the beginning. For example, I'm so scared to tell my spouse or sibling they are driving me crazy because I do not want to fight or make her/him angry. What happens? It builds and builds and then blows up. Instead, imagine approaching this with love and explaining what is driving you crazy. It's hypothetical here; however, the approach and landing are critical, much like an airplane to success. Are you more fearful of facing fear and overcoming or living in fear? I have been guilty of both. That emotion drives your life and stays in you should you not get it out.

Fear is an emotion you must conquer to be happy in life. Fear stifles your growth in all areas and makes you an inner prisoner of your mind. Facing fear conveys that you are healthy and are confident in yourself, much like going to the dentist, most of us are fearful, however, the outcome, should we have prepared and taken care of our teeth is positive. It's the same with facing our fears in life.

As I stated in my opening, I was fearful of many things in life, even publishing this book. However, I realized that I was more afraid of not publishing it. I believed in myself and said whatever the outcome or response, should I help one person it will be a success. I overcame my fear, just like you can. Facing fear opens many different emotions and doors along the way. Understand the feeling you have, accept it, and then figure out what the driving factor is. Facing your fears will set you free.

When we were children, say two, three years old, before all the brain wiring, we were not fearful of anything except loud noises and heights. We didn't judge people by their gender, skin color, money, opinion, looks, height, abilities, name it, and just accepting them. We didn't break it all down and soaked in the wonderment of it all. That is why you must search what you are fearful of and return to the two-year-old mentality of why; accept it and conquer it. When you face your fears in life and overcome them, you become very powerful inside, and you grow exponentially.

Fear that builds from others' actions is just evil at work—a dark force attempting to get you to churn and get you off your path to happiness. Your fears are like water; it flows to the lowest place. You feel frustrated with your most inferior thoughts-you are attacked through them. Instead, face your fears head-on, conquer them all, and use the knowledge you gain from this for strength to settle the conflict(s). Use the power of love to overcome all fears. Use that power to help others face their fears. Be their mirror of light on the shining hill of life. Show others they can overcome anything. Once you relinquish fear and start living life by Rule #1, having fun no matter what you do, you will find that your life will be happier and filled with less fear.

Someone once told me, "run to your fears," which I interpret as conquering your fears. When we face ourselves in our mirror and determine why we fear what you do. Whatever you are afraid of, besides the obvious things that will hurt you, conquer. Take a flight somewhere by yourself, ask that person you adore to dinner, go dancing, talk to your spouse or companion about what's bothering you or them. Do something to move past whatever you fear and start living. The truth will always set you free.

Overcoming whatever you fear will set you free. You will no longer be a prisoner. It will raise your vibration by changing the fear of a growth mechanism in your life. You will have overcome fear. That is an achievement that makes you proud, which increases your energy. Your aura will change, and people will notice it. Your energy will then not attract fearful, negative people; you will attract positive, outgoing people. You will be in good company. Fear likes the company, much like anger, drama, or guilt. Fear is a negative emotion that will destroy you and your future. Face it and turn it into a positive. Learn from fear. Turn the table on fear. Make fear a lap dog in your reality, a friendly, cute, little thing that you do not fear. You will learn many lessons.

LOVE

"You have to love yourself before others can love you."
– The Universe

Whether you believe it not, we are all searching for love, all different forms of love. There are many kinds of love, such as maternal, familial, romantic, marital, plutonic, and so on. Most times, our love for one another makes us overlook each other's faults and shortcomings. And sometimes we lie awake at night or daydream, searching for love's answers. Love takes many forms, which is why it's tough to define. We all have some unique solutions to what we think love is. It's different for everyone; however, love, real love is the same for us all. Love means that you care for another living thing just as much or more than yourself. Or is that love? Is love a response to someone or something that makes us identify with good? Is love an attachment to an experience? Is real love between children and their parents? What the heck is love? Let's scratch the surface.

    As a building needs a foundation, so does love, and the foundation of love can be very complicated or very simple. Love does not always show itself today; however, there and ready to be cultivated should people take enough time and interest to do so. That brings us to the meaning of love. As humans, we have two emotions, love, and fear; it's the light and the dark. Love isn't a tangible thing; it's a powerful emotion that drives our lives. As Osho states in the book; Life is a Soap Bubble: 100 ways to look at Life, "Love is fearless. The absence of love is fear. Someone who wants to transcend fear will have to become full of love for the existence. From one door of consciousness, love enters; from the other, fear exits." Love is the emotion that binds us all together in perfect harmony. It is the love of our parents that is the foundation. A mother's and a father's love are irreplaceable and priceless for a child. That love shapes our subconscious and later outlook on love and life. As stated, love takes on many forms, and we experience love in our way. So, what is love?

Love is a potent emotion. Love is involuntary; it happens in many ways. A power that overtakes us with an attraction that craves for the same. You must love yourself before others can love you. In romantic love, love is about compatibility. Men and women start at such different points of view about almost everything in life; we are programmed differently. However, when we conclude on solving something together as one, it's beautiful. It's a collection of both sides that comes to a perfect circle. The love between a man and a woman or any other type of romantic relationship is the toughest thing most of us will face in life besides parenting. And at the same time, it can be the most beautiful thing should that love be shared. Love is the most powerful emotion you will ever experience in life. It's like that King's X song, "It's Love," should you like rock, I recommend this song. A strong emotion that can make you do and accomplish things you never thought you would do. Love can make you very happy or in the wrong relationship make you very crazy. It's a leap of faith that you take and put your whole self out there for someone else, noble, and reciprocated. It's the outcome that will shape you as a person.

Finding the one, finding Mr. or Mrs. Right is a myth. Nobody is perfect; we all have faults. The question is, are we right for each other? We all need some guidance in love, all forms of love, nobody is a complete expert. Connecting to the universe and the unconditional love is the beginning. Once you join and you use love wisely and find someone who can deal with your issues. You can deal with their problems, forgive quickly, are comfortable in all situations, accept them for who they are, trust them, do not attempt to change them, and enjoy being in each other's company, that's love. Should you love someone, all you need is the air you breathe.

Struggles in life and relationships should bring you closer together to fix an issue. Every battle you overcome allows you to learn something about yourself or another and not fear it anymore. These struggles with our parents, kids, friends, and partners open another level of love through respect and understanding. When talking through whatever issue and understanding that we are not perfect, the imperfections will smooth out to bring out the love we have for one another. Sometimes we experience things differently than others due to our background, childhood, love, and relationship history. Do your best to make your loved ones feel loved by your thoughtful actions and words. Share decisions and be honest with them and yourself. Love is about forgiveness, trust, and honesty. Using love to solve your issues with yourself and others allows struggles to be resolved peacefully. That shows that you not only love that person, that you also love yourself.

Our entire existence on this earth is to share our love with others and have them share their passion with us. Love is the ability to connect with other people who want to be loved (very important, to want to be loved and to love) as moms, dads, children, friends, companions, wives, husbands, girlfriends, and boyfriends. We should strive to surround ourselves with these loving people. Not all people understand love; some need help. Love can change your whole outlook on life. Learn how to love and love completely. Having and finding people who love and care about you is the ultimate answer to conquering and expelling life's fears. Love is a compelling emotion that can be the most beautiful experience. Learn what love is and build the foundation of love through trust. Apply real love to people, pay attention to their actions, their words, set the correct expectations, maintain your right side of the relationship. You will find the ultimate experience of life. Love!!!

FINDING YOURSELF

"Knowing yourself is the beginning of all wisdom."
– Aristotle

What is Aristotle stating? I believe he is explaining the path to wisdom. It's a journey for everyone to search within and figure out their meaning in life. We are always under construction to build ourselves to a higher place. Actively nurturing a sturdy foundation or pouring a new stable one to continue our journey. Striving to become enlightened to the real meaning of life, know ourselves, and not let others define who we are— like the vine, allowing our dreams to become the blossoms. The worm that becomes the beautiful butterfly and the fertile roots to grow the abundant fruit tree that produces love, joy, and happiness. Working on letting go of negative thoughts about ourselves and displaying our beauty into the world. Visualizing our dreams and making them become a reality, recognizing the hardships and overcoming them, and continually learning the lessons and where they are taking us. That's the path to finding yourself.

According to me, knowing yourself means recognizing your downfalls, your good qualities, your self-value, your self-love, your soul, and the life lessons you have experienced. The knowledge we incorporate into our life from these lessons that allow us to learn from them. Should you not know yourself, who do you know? That's how you find yourself. It's a quest to find yourself. Sometimes we find out how foolish we have been. I am a man; trust me. That's okay; at least we can change that behavior. You wonder, who is the bigger fool, the fool or the one who follows the fool? However, when we find our self and channel our energy to our dreams, the world is our oyster. There is only one relationship that can change our life, that's the relationship with ourselves. There is only one relationship we will have our entire life, which is the relationship with our self. All others will end, good or bad, or by death, however, they will end. We can either be our best friend or our worst enemy.

After wandering through life and not entirely knowing how I got where I'm at or who I was, my journey was elevated by many people, many downfalls, and many moments. I'll focus on a person that made something click. He was brilliant and had a terrible disease. He was a millionaire who now lives on the streets of Austin, Texas. He was a friend who lost his mind, money, and family. He lived with me for thirty days, and I tell you, it was eye-opening on many levels. He not only made me explore my inner thoughts and how I thought but made me challenge myself. He would make signs and post them on the bathroom mirror and the refrigerator. They read, "You are Special," "You will be President of the United States one day," and never use these words ever again Anakin (Star Wars reference) "If, Can't, Try, But, Might," which I do not to this day. Every day was draining. Not until after I dropped him off at one of his friend's house and was reflecting weeks later did I realize what he did for me? He jarred something and changed me or changed how I perceived me. He changed me by making me pay attention to my words, actions, and thoughts. He made me look within for all my life's answers. He seeded my spiritual journey within.

Why did I learn from this guy? The answers flooded in, and I began to learn about myself. I learned that everybody has a different past and a different genetic makeup. I learned that because I think a certain way that everybody else does not feel the same way. I learned how to forgive myself for making mistakes and how to love myself. I reflected within and opened to the universe. I realized what most people do in life and what I did is to think people should be a certain way, act a certain way, react a certain way, however, when they do not, it causes us to become upset. I corrected that. I found that when I thought someone did something wrong, I didn't need an apology; they owed me nothing. They did not believe they did anything wrong. I learned to let go and not become angry instead to forgive.

Huge step there. I was not a prisoner anymore. No one owed me an apology for anything. I found that living in reality, real reality, not what I think reality is, and operating in reality not only brings clarity to situations, it also brings clarity to life, real life. I connected to myself. I began looking past my subconscious and making my conscious thoughts a reality. That's what you must do to find yourself; you must open your mind to a different way of thinking about yourself. The power of positive, loving, real thought can change your entire life. Are you thinking now?

Nobody cares about your excuses. You may think they do; however, they don't give a darn. It's your perception versus reality. Again, relative to the situation and relationship. Most people I surrounded myself with at the time kept heading in the same direction in life and never reflected in themselves. They would go through the motions and medicated their issues with substances, not everyone, most of them, though. They would go back to the same old pattern. So, when I would receive this text message on my phone, "Hey, want to grab a drink?" I started paying attention to how I acted. It didn't go well at first, I would drink a bunch, wake up with a hangover and start thinking, what am I doing, again? Then work all week, forget, and you guessed it, rinse and repeat. I continued this vicious cycle for a while with some circles of people and perceived friends. Nobody but myself was at fault here; I just didn't want to change; it was too comfortable being that guy. However, one day I clicked, saw the whole charade, grew inside, and realized it. I saw my future. It was bright, and I had to just to let go of the things inside that made me do this. I then began the process to challenge myself and get out of the "bubble" and act as my heart told me. We'll explore the bubble in a bit. To go to places with people who made me feel good, appreciated, and loved. I realized hanging out with people whom I had a dysfunctional relationship with was moving backward in life.

It was crazy the outcome when I started doing this. People around me would say things like, should there be a nuclear war, only three things will exist, roaches, plastic, and hopefully a cool guy like you to rebuild the planet. What the heck? Or, an older gentleman told me one day at the pool, everyone loves you here, all the woman, men, kids, everyone. This place would not exist without you. It was amazing. When you change yourself and think from the spirit instead of the flesh, a whole new world will open. Just like what you can do with your life, remove the obstacles that poison your soul, or cloud your destiny. Follow the true spirit inside you instead of leading you to wholeness.

We face these challenges as a collective society and have no idea what to do next. That is why you may be reading this book. That is why you may have begun your journey to face yourself and conquer your demons. To consciously reflect into yourself and fight the fear or anxiety and overcome. When we do this, we learn about ourselves and apply good things and leave the bad ones behind. Looking through that mirror of life allows you to meditate about yourself, understand your emotions, isolate the thoughts you use to hold yourself back and overcome them. Learn to end self-destructive thoughts, reflect on the mistakes and the victories. Correct them and praise them. This action will allow you to find yourself and set yourself free.

Finding yourself is a journey that can span an entire lifetime. Starting early, however, is a path to happiness. Getting to know yourself is a profound reflection within that can be very scary. Most people go through life and never do this. They never remove the silly things our minds flood us with every day. They never understand what and who they are or where they are going; they allow others to determine that. They enable their faults and others to drain their energy. They let their ego to feed them with false narratives. Learn to change these negative thoughts and channel your energy to positive thoughts about yourself and your dreams. End the practice of allowing your energy to flow towards bad relationships or friends or people who do not love and care about you. Relationships will end, and sorrows will happen to you along the way, grow from them, do not allow the negative to destroy you. Use the energy to propel you forward. Then do not fall prey and allow possessions like fancy cars, houses, and clothes to cloud your identity and determine your worthiness. You are already worthy without this stuff once you realize and connect with your soul. Understand you can lose all these possessions, then, where are you? You make you, not anyone else, and make you happy by finding, loving, and connecting with yourself.

Your value is already inside you, and it's the purest thing you own. It's your soul. That understanding propels you. Then, no matter what situation or hardships you encounter, you can move forward in life without the attachment to the material things or people's opinions. Remember that Sting song, "We are Spirits in the Material World?" Understand that's all we are and search within yourself. You may find things you do not like, address, and get rid of them. Build on the good qualities. Search what your real dreams are and what you want your life to be, visualize it, write it down, manifest it, and work towards it— allowing you to achieve happiness to attract what you are seeking in life. You will have found out who you are and what makes you tick.

When you are genuine and generous, you will see the abundance in return. That energy will spread to the people you love by your actions. The energy will increase within all your circles of friends and family, making them happy, spreading worth, and making everybody feel loved. It may even change people. It's funny to see someone's face turn from anger to love; it's magical. And to see someone's heart change from hatred to love. It's a feeling of such a connection with their soul and the universe to become loving versus selfish.

Like the universe and what you are striving for in your relationship with yourself and others, complete balance. When you use loving actions and thoughts to solve your life, you not only find yourself but also find love for yourself. The love of self and the karmic lessons will be understood. The internal search will expose the wrong things, but it will reveal the good ones too. Release bad ones and nurture the good ones. Finding out who you are will set you free in today's society. Understand the realities that most people you interact with have no clue who they are or where their life is taking them. They live in the 2D, 3D world of reality shows, judging people, arguing politics or sports, chasing the flesh or thinking money is more important than the love of family, love of self and love of life itself. Allow love to guide you to your purpose and find yourself. When you understand that the only thing that matters in life is love, people, and the love of people, you will not only understand the law of life and the universe but also understand yourself.

LOVING YOURSELF

"You yourself, as much as anybody in the entire universe, deserve your love and affection."
– Buddha

I highly recommend you read about Buddha's and his teachings. Do we not automatically love ourselves? Do you? How do you love yourself? Loving yourself is a conscious thought. It means choosing the right ideas, words, knowledge, actions, foods, health level, attitude, and planning. You end the practice of looking at yourself the way the world or people see you; you look at yourself how the universe sees you; beautiful and unique with the ability to do whatever you believe in your mind. Upon reflecting on myself on how I saw the world, bluntly, I started caring for myself. I had shied away from enjoying life as I felt sorry for myself due to my brother passing away when I was seventeen. I chose to live this way. It is eye-opening and enlightening when I realized nothing matters in life except what you will think about on your death bed, to a certain extent. I let go and learned everything happened for a reason; it's not up to me to figure that out. When I began to move on and love myself wholly, I began to understand the true meaning of life. The unconditional love of thyself.

I began by addressing my issues, such as lust, jealousy, fear, desires, self-doubt, and my brother's death. I turned it around in my mind. I made the right decisions about myself most of the time. I got in shape; I changed my diet. I ran ten to twelve miles a week, worked out at the gym five days a week, and lost over fifty pounds. I was doing this for me. Yes, me, me!!! Big step. You must be happy on the inside for your body to look and perform its best! It's always best to do things for others. However, you must do something for yourself first, much like securing the oxygen mask that drops in an airplane should that ever happen to you. You must love yourself before others can love you.

I then began to branch outside and talk with people I knew, or I would find myself interacting with strangers, people at the grocery store, work, volleyball guys, women, old folks, young people at the gym, you name it. I found out that we all have issues, pasts, and things we cannot let go of that creep into our minds daily, sabotaging our happiness. We all have issues and crosses to bear. I understood I was not alone and began to surrender all the drama. I recognized the emotions from those hardships and addressed them. Love for the self is the journey. Let's see how we can begin to love ourselves.

Loving yourself takes some steps to achieve. The beginning is learning to forgive yourself and treasure yourself. You and your soul are as unique as a snowflake, embrace that. This will set you free of all the self-doubt. Working on forgiving yourself for past life events such as anger, being jealous, saying hateful things, hurting others, and all the things you think you have done wrong or wrongs against you. That is the past, let it go. You cannot go back, and that is not who you are today. Call the people you felt you hurt and ask for forgiveness. Then forgive others, let the universe and karma deal with them. By living this way, you open to all forms of forgiveness. You open to the present. Next, stop taking yourself so darn seriously. It's easy today to get caught up in the world around us that you lose your humor, no one likes everything to be so severe. There is a time and place for everything, though. Stay positive and away from the negative aspects of today's life, like the news, a bad friend or relative, a bad relationship, instead tell jokes or read/watch something funny or educational.

Another step is to stop identifying with suffering or a loss as being you. I did with my brother's death and my divorce, what a disaster and a waste of time and life. When you relieve yourself of these negative thoughts and associations, the real you has a chance to blossom. Your happiness returns, and you attract what you want to fill the hole inside you. As we will discuss later, be yourself, your true self with all the perceived blemishes. Pure perfection is accepting your imperfections. When you learn to accept yourself completely and who you are, even the things you do not like, you release yourself from the inner struggle of self-rejection. You stop worrying about how you look when you go somewhere and have a good time. You stop comparing yourself to others for their beauty, clothes, or the people that surround them. We are all unique; there is no one on this planet like you, recognize that and your greatness. Become your greatest friend. The relationship you have with yourself is the only one that will last your entire lifetime. Stay positive with yourself.

Then, begin the practice of not emotionally draining yourself by putting yourself down and beating yourself up. It's okay to laugh at yourself. Trust me, laughing at the dumb things you have done is refreshing in the right environment. Be kind to yourself and others. Recognize your emotions; it's easy to repress emotions when they seem overwhelming; however, should you honor it, it will bring you closer to the inner happiness beneath the suffering or grief. When you acknowledge and make friends with your genuine emotions, you understand forgiving yourself is one of the greatest gifts of life. Lastly, meditate. Just get comfortable somewhere quiet for five minutes and close your eyes. Follow your breath. Meditation is associated with changes in the brain associated with happiness and contentment. It promotes the area of our brain that makes us feel good about who we are and who we are becoming. Meditating on a future goal, love, kindness, forgiveness for examples will make you happier. Lastly, walk barefoot on the earth, not in shoes and on the pavement, on the grass-connects you to the planet, and sends healthy energy through you. Practice these ideas and see where it takes you, hopefully to inner peace and self-love.

We will never physically see the higher power; some belief in here on earth until, should you believe in the rapture, he will appear and raise all the believers and leave the non-believers to doom and gloom. However, we will see the higher power's unconditional love through other people's actions and words once you recognize it. That is the same for you, no one will ever see inside you, except you. You need to become your own Lord. Only you can save you, no one else will. You need to change the way you think about yourself should any of it be negative. Do it from the heart. Build yourself up every day and think about how I can make myself better. Allowing yourself to visualize what your dreams are and putting them into action will enable you to experience happiness. It allows you to love yourself and understand where your life's future is. Realize that everything you put into your body reflects you, including knowledge. You are your biggest fan, start thinking that every day. Are you thinking?

I have people at work that stop by my desk to talk about things, randomly, which I find interesting. I just say something, and off they go. I spoke with a guy one day about many topics, and self-love came up out of nowhere. It was the day after some guy shot up a church Southeast of San Antonio, Texas. We touched on a few things and then began a discussion about loving yourself. How does that happen? I will tell you; you sit back and analyze why people do things. I'll cut to the chase; the shooter didn't love himself or anyone else. His ego overtook him because his girlfriend left him. Remember, these relationships happen and are part of the path, a test. Learn from them, take from the negative, and turn it into positive energy. The other route is very destructive to your health and your soul. You will have to relive the lesson again.

I was out at the ranch later that week and spoke to a guy that I would never have thought about his life, wife, and where they were headed. He was shocked when I told him that he smoked like a chimney and drank beer like no tomorrow and said you do not love yourself. He sat there and stared into my eyes like a deer in headlights. As we continued, he slowly understood what I was telling him. When I went back to the cabin, he sat alone and began to rewire his brain to see the world differently to see a different side of himself. I know this because he starred off into the distance; you know that hundred-mile stare. A few weeks later, he said he and his wife had worked it out, and he was moving home. He reflected within, just like you can do. Everyone you meet is your mirror in life, pay attention to what they tell you, it just may change your perception of yourself.

Towards the end of writing this book, I had a co-worker whose husband did the unthinkable; I was unaware of the situation. She was distraught a bit at work, and I just minded my own business, remember I am good at that. One day I was working late, and she asked whether she could speak to me about something. I said, sure, and it started almost immediately with tears. I was a bit shocked. However, I knew her and knew she was suffering. I listened and was heartbroken for her. I felt my heart tearing for this young woman. She told me she was this way and that way and said, "what should I do?" I said this would be the hardest test so far in your life and you are young, use love and see where it takes you. Remember to love yourself through the process, as this can be a rough road of escaping through bad behaviors.

I then said the hardest thing to do is the right thing all the time, no matter how someone treats you. We discussed ideas for thirty minutes, and she would try. I said, "Do or do not; there is no try." Yes, that's Yoda. A few days later, she told me that they sat down and worked through everything, they started going to therapy, and they were not getting back together anytime soon; however, they had addressed the real issues due to using love instead of anger. I was happy for her. By using love in her discussions that night with her soon to be ex-husband, she may not have gotten the result she wanted. Sometimes it takes time; however, by demonstrating that she loved herself by talking things over and showing him forgiveness, they now have a new beginning. And sometimes, a new beginning is about someone else learning to love themselves to understand. Never give up on love, and never give up loving yourself. It will change your life!

Loving yourself lives in your mind, body, and soul. It's displayed to others by your actions, well-being, and what you say when communicating. The perception of others about you is an illumination about what you think about your inner self. You do not have to prove yourself when you love yourself. You may lose your job, your money, your house, your significant other, and then, where are you? Is that your worth? Is it all about other's people's approval and material possessions? When you live this way, you will never be satisfied. You will be chasing people and their consent your entire life—an endless journey.

Your worthiness is inside you already; it's your soul. You clean up the inside by learning your lessons, understanding your karma, and releasing the negative emotions that you may harbor. Shine the light of love on the darkness inside you by acknowledging you made a mistake or that someone hurt you. Call them up or let it go. When you address these thoughts that keep you a prisoner and overcome them, you will become whole, and joy will fill your heart. You will feel free. When you get out of the way and trust the universe's plan for you, you achieve happiness and self-love.

Fill your mind with self-love and love for others. Eat well, get in shape, exercise your mind with knowledge, find love in your soul, and change your outlook. Your life will change! You will feel better about all aspects of life as you will be healthier on all levels. That will allow you to branch outside your comfort zone, run a 5K, walk the beach for hours, or take your kids/grandkids to the zoo and not be tired walking around. Instead, your focus will be on the glory of the place and building memories. The purity of thought allows you to raise your vibration, and when you do, you attract the same beautiful energy. Once you accomplish loving yourself, others will be drawn to the aura that surrounds you. You will be happy with yourself, and you will stop beating yourself up for anything. Then you will find your true happiness in your heart and your life. Start loving yourself!!!

Pay Attention

*"Pay attention to the things you are naturally drawn to. They are often connected to your path, passion, and purpose in life.
Have the courage to follow them."*
– Ruben Chavez

Ever felt something or a voice inside tell you to do something? Did you listen? Do you hear your spirit? Listening to our inner self is something we all should think about at some time in our life. We must pay attention to the messages we receive from the internal. When we follow that inside voice, we find our destiny. We understand where to focus our energy and the people we should surround ourselves with every day. We gain an understanding of our meaning in this lifetime. I lived unaware of this practice for most of my life. When you pay attention to all the internal messages, you will start to notice your life changes on the outside, trust me.

Paying attention is described as awareness, mindfulness, concentration. Defined as to listen to, watch, or consider something or someone very carefully. Most people never pay attention to their inner voice or the many messages the universe sends us. They never even think about their life purpose. They're way too busy, working, checking social media, playing on their smartphone, in a dysfunctional relationship, and on and on. They only pay attention to the external. They do not listen to the messages. When we step back from the 3D world and pay attention to these messages, we understand our life's direction. Our job is to decipher the messages and follow them.

You and I receive messages all the time—many of them, through everyday experiences, collect them through recurring experiences, dreams, animals, patterns of numbers, or objects; Déjà vu. They occur through recurring words and phrases, pain and illness, songs, the weather, and unexpected meetings. We sense them though emotions that are out of place, unusual words, smells, and gut feelings. However, many of us are too busy these days to pay attention to them. We have better things to do. Instead, begin to write down and study these messages. They will have a profound message to what you have been seeking.

On a human level, I found the truth is stranger than fiction. Many people these days fool themselves and live in the churn. The churn is the constant speed, societal pressures, emphasis on money, lack of respect and values, constantly checking smartphones, chasing the flesh, and the stress this causes. They only pay attention to their thoughts and emotions—the 3D world. For example, I dislike my job; I'm broke, someone is cheating on me; everything is an emergency for my significant other, you name it. They get lost. People get lost; they stop paying attention to everything. They lose sight of their weight, their health, their loved ones, their job, driving. You name it. They allow the external to consume their thoughts, and they never listen to their heart. By tuning into ourselves, we hear and act on the messages from our hearts. We channel our energy towards ourselves and the people we love.

It's easy to live offended and upset; anyone can do this. It's easy to go out and get drunk or get on drugs. Becoming the eagle that flies above all the storms and drama is the tough road. The hard part is doing the right thing all the time. However, when you practice this, the churn disappears, no one is harassing you, and you can sleep at night. You leave the drama of the world to other people and television. You can prepare for your life and your dreams. You can pay attention to your heart and channel your energy towards you. You begin to pay attention to where your life is heading and where you want it to go.

You are unable to change anyone; you can only change yourself. Instead of changing the world, start by changing yourself and making yourself happy. Do you think all those protestors fighting in the streets over whatever are happy? Do you think they allow somebody else to control their emotions? Their life? Do you think they will ever be satisfied? They are chasing the past. They are seeking change to anything they feel needs to be changed ill regardless of what others think. They are upset at society due to bad parenting or the poor education they received. You can only change you into the present, not your past. As the old saying goes, "universe, grant me the serenity to accept the things I cannot change, courage to change the things I can, and the wisdom to know the difference." By paying attention to your life and the lives of the people you love, you can change your environment and your future.

By living your conscious life in the moment, you live in the truth. Paying attention allows you to grow in many ways. It leads you to the internal and away from the drama of the 3D world. In the article, Attention by Frederic and Mary Ann Brussat, they state, "Eventually, without awareness, we end up living in a daze of stimulation without any grasp of its significance. We operate on automatic pilot without even realizing it. Nothing registers on our consciousness; we feel drained of energy. However, not paying attention has the opposite effect: everything registers, and we don't know what to do with it all. We are bombarded with stimuli, and we can't focus on anything. We feel scattered. We stress out. For both lack of energy and stress, paying attention is a good corrective prescription." To decipher, we need to pay attention to our lives, our souls' voices, and act on it.

Our soul leads us to happiness. We must end the practice that the external world is the stimuli. When we reverse this process and allow our focus to the inside of us, we achieve awareness. When we follow those intuitive messages, beautiful things begin to happen. Our life is not so clouded; we begin to understand the messages and act. We leave the ego's nagging voice behind. We know the universe is in control. We have favor to achieve what we have longed for our entire lives, our life's meaning.

At this point in history, we cannot go back in time, which is why you need preparation. When you keep churning, who is the life prisoner? Should you want to change the pattern, then develop and improve yourself. Some people, however, struggle daily because they never release the past. They have never learned to forgive. Sometimes, even the darkest wrongs of justice committed on someone require therapy and work. I am not brushing aside the reality that bad things happen to people. We all need to find a way to release the negative energy inside of us and let go. The karma this action creates needs to be released before we can become whole and balanced.

Paying attention to our connection with ourselves not only guides us; it helps others. I saved a guy's life once by paying attention to my inner self. The story goes like this. One beautiful Sunday morning, I walked to the gym to work out as I usually did. Nothing out of the ordinary. I arrived early, and the gym was empty. The sun was shining through the windows and lit the floor with a golden orange color. I looked over and saw this big guy over by the squat rack. He was lifting some hefty weight, around three-hundred and fifteen pounds, I believe. I introduced myself and said, "Wow dude, that is a lot of weight, did you play football in college?" He said he was from Pittsburg, Pennsylvania, and played high school football twenty years ago. We chatted, and I said, have a great workout. I went to do my core exercises for thirty minutes, then lifted for about an hour. When I finished, I went into the men's locker room, changed and washed up a bit. When I came out, the big guy I had spoken to had collapsed on the floor under the water fountain. There was a young guy behind the desk, and his eyes were wide open, much like an owl's. I then had a gut feeling come over me, the little voice inside, telling me to take care of him. No one except the guy behind the desk and me was paying attention to him.

I asked him a few questions, and he had trouble speaking. He said his chest hurt. I said, "We are calling an ambulance," he said, "no," you know, tough-guy stuff. I said, "You have one minute." A minute in and this guy's eyes roll back, and he is in excruciating pain. I tell the young guy to call 911. The little voice said to get a cloth out of the closet and put cold water on it. The water fountain was right above him. I then placed the towel on his forehead. I tell him every ten seconds that he is doing great and will be fine. The cold cloth heats up quickly as he begins sweating. I keep repeating the process. I had no idea what was telling me to do this.

Now there are five people, paying attention, and start crowding in on us. In a calm voice, I tell everyone to back up and go back to working out. We have this covered. This situation continues for about eight minutes, and some paramedics show up. They take over the job. I ask the guy on the floor who to call, take his phone and call his buddy. To this day, his buddy has never called me back. I get his keys and grab his wallet out of his car. I escorted the guy and the paramedics to the ambulance, give them his keys and wallet, and sit in there with him. We are there for about five minutes, and the paramedics say, "he has a heart attack, we need to go." I said, "I told him I would be with him all the way," the paramedic just said, "it will not help." I got out of the ambulance, and they took off. I text the young guy from the gym later in the day, and he had stopped by the hospital and saw the guy.

Fast forward to Monday, the next day; I go to the gym after work. I walk in, and the girl behind the counter says, "You saved his life." I said, "really?" She said, "yes, we have the whole incident on tape. He called and should you have not done everything that you did that he would be dead. The doctor told him this." Wow, the emotion that overcame me. He had a heart attack and two stints put into the two arteries leading to his heart as they were clogged. I went about my life and saw him a few weeks later, and he thanked me, subtly. Which is all I needed; I wasn't after anything. I saved this guy's life by paying attention to what the universe told. I had listened to my inner self. That is what I am asking you to do.

Paying attention to our life, the ones we love, and the signs from the universe are essential to achieving our dreams. It increases our knowledge and our ability to interact, help, and understand people. It enables us to develop us. It helped me save someone's life; I know this is extreme; however, paying attention in life can also save yours from despair. Begin to pay attention to everything in your life! Pay attention when driving, pay attention to your spouse or significant other, pay attention to your kids, pay attention to your parents, pay attention to your thoughts, pay attention to your health. Pay attention to your connection with the universe and your soul, as they are the guiding principle. It will guide you to what you seek and happiness. Paying attention allows you to enlighten yourself to enjoy every day and everyone in your life. By paying attention, you can change your life and your loved one's lives. Paying attention to the inside of yourself will lead you to your life purpose.

LIVING IN THE PRESENT

"Do not dwell in the past; do not dream of the future, concentrate the mind on the present moment."
– Buddha

Why do you keep mentioning living in the present? What is it? Why is this so important? Living in the present is being aware of what flows through your senses as they are happening. Understanding and paying attention to the moment. The truth. You are the director of your life movie. Time is an illusion. We are drawn into the past or the future, or both. Surrender to what is right now and commit to being there, completely. Life will take care of the rest. That is living in the present.

We all let our minds wander, which is excellent; however, sometimes that can cause trouble and bring on emotions like stress, fear, guilt, anxiety, and many more. When we allow ourselves to live in our past, our present situation is blinding by these thoughts. We are distracted around others due to their effect on our psyche. When they are negative emotions or fearful thoughts, our body releases serotonin as though we are experiencing a real situation. It's stress on our body and organs. Living in the present allows us to pay attention to what is going on around us. It enables us to absorb the beauty of the world and the experiences with the people to remember and make lasting memories. By forgiving ourselves of the past, we experience the present moment. We learn to live life in a world of the now. That action increases our energy by connecting us to all living things and the universe. It allows us to enjoy the moment.

Living in the present has a direct effect on our emotional well-being and physical health. Mental and emotional stress is a huge factor in society today and impacts many of us. When we step back from our thoughts and live in the moment, the universe favors us; it connects us with the energy. We all have an inner voice and believe in what we want our lives to be. Along the way, we allow our minds to cloud our inner voice of our soul. We allow our egoic thoughts to take us out of the present. When we recognize these thoughts that go against the faith inside us, we learn not to let our minds talk us out of the present. We develop a conscious awareness that is paying attention, and we release the past. We allow peace in our life, love in our hearts, and the strength to forgive others. We understand our history, accept it, and are not distracted by those negative thoughts. We learn to release people who do not bring us growth anymore. We learn to forgive them, and we begin to live a fruitful life in the present.

We all struggle with this situation from day to day to stay present in our minds. It takes practice and forgiveness to get there. Instead, we should build our thoughts about our lives and look to a positive future filled with the dreams we have manifested for ourselves. When we pay attention to our surroundings, we understand what is going on around us. We are not living in another world unless you go around everywhere, staring at your smartphone. End the practice of worrying about other people's lives, social media, and channel your energy to your life.

We have received the gifts of our senses, most of us, and allow them to sometimes keep us from not living in the present. I have been very guilty of this by interrupting someone speaking because I think I already know what they are going to say. Someone once told me "You have two ears and one mouth, which means you can listen and learn twice the amount should keep your mouth shut." Allow others to speak their thoughts entirely and then engage. Allow others to express their beliefs without getting angry completely should it go against what you believe. Separate their opinions from the person as I think most people are good. It allows everyone to live in the present instead of someone racing off about thoughts of how much of a jerk I was, or you may have been. Pay attention to these things. Use your mind, not your ego.

Believing in yourself and living in the present will bring you what you seek and exceed your expectations. Your dreams are already inside you. Believe in yourself, your goals, visualize them, and act on them. Do not talk yourself out of them. You will be surprised by the abundance the universe will deliver. You will see the clarity of your destiny and get out of any dysfunction in your life. Listen to that inner voice, your energy, and your soul guiding you.

Live in the present and all its glory and gifts. Breathe in all the experiences. When you experience anxiety, connect with your breath, connect to the universe, and dig in to figure out why. Practice training yourself to overcome fearful thoughts that may flood in when speaking in public or meeting someone new, for example. Soak up those experiences instead with your eyes experience the excitement. Use the voice inside to guide your thoughts and words with confidence. Remember, you must believe in yourself before anyone else will. Understand and use the love in your heart once you have connected to a higher power to empower yourself and others to accomplish anything in life. No matter how big. You must dream big. How do you think someone like Jeff Bezos created Amazon? Fear? Or did he overcome fear? When you do these things, you will receive more in life than you have ever imagined. You will receive all the gifts of living in the present. Incredibly, just one change in your life will not only change you; it will change everyone around you. Living in the present will allow your mind to pay attention to the essential things that matter in life and understand your journey. We are all on one magical ride, make yours count for what you want it to be. How beautiful!

Bubble to Bubble

*"The best things in life are often waiting for you
at the exit ramp of your comfort zone"*
– Karen Salmansohn

Bubble to bubble as I have explained with visual hand gestures to people, yes, you can visualize it now, is not staying in the same frame of mind to keep growing and enriching our life. Use many frames of reference. Look out all the windows of the building, not just one, when searching for the answers. It's the ability to change a thought to a different, hopefully, positive about an event or our past. Consciously move to a different opinion about an unpleasant emotion. Analyze from outside "the bubble" inside our heart and mind, to learn about a social group, a person, or our self. Think about the unseen instead of the recorded visual actions or words of an event. Stop playing the same old record and move on to the new soundtrack. Step outside "the bubble" and analyze the situation to figure out the cause of the issue. Learn to forgive the who or what and our self. Remove any negative emotion from an event and look within to change the record permanently. Change our thoughts on the way we perceive our past, future, self, and others.

I've played water volleyball for over twenty years. Every summer weekend, I proceeded to the pool and did the same thing. I occasionally would miss a weekend to go fishing or do some work out at the ranch, or go on a trip; however, that was my life, my "comfort zone." I met some many new people, however, the same ole folks. When I began to pay attention and analyze the whole atmosphere, I had no idea what I was doing or what others were doing down there; it never crossed my mind. I never realized how dysfunctional some aspects were. However, over a whole summer, I reflected and observed in my mind "outside the bubble" at the mayhem. I watched the social issues playing out in front of me and all the crazy antics. It appears people were upset in life and took it out on others or consumed way too much alcohol. By the way, me too. I noticed many things about myself and others. I saw many of the guys were not having fun and were becoming upset at the way we interacted and played water volleyball against each other. I then thought about how this could all change for the better. Slowly, I changed my thoughts and actions.

I changed myself and how I thought about the whole place. I remember reading about how using loving actions can change everything. I searched within, and the answers flooded in. I received the wisdom that I didn't need to speak and act like everyone else anymore. I learned to be the light in the dark world we live in now. I enacted the peace with the way I interacted with others and myself. I begin using loving actions and words on and off the court to the best of my ability. I had jumped to another bubble or thought. I changed the record for everyone at the pool and the music genre to an upbeat, positive vibe. I just looked in from the outside within myself. It was a fantastic outcome. The whole place changed, and so did I. It was beautiful and fun. It was exciting, full of positive energy and loving actions. People began to bring a great attitude. It was wonderful. That is how you train your mind to grow and correct issues in "your bubble."

Living my life, doing the same things over and over, same restaurant, same bar, same friends, same vacations, same everything gets you in a rut and not excited about the future. You must be passionate about your future and get out of your proverbial "comfort zone" to experience things in life to keep growing. To live a happy life, you need to get out of your bubble and experience the world around you. When you experience different things, taste different foods, see different places, meet different people, and face your fears, you learn. That's what it's all about, changing the internal record, conquering your fears and letting go of all the non-growth mechanisms in your life. You will have an explosive development period. You will understand your connection to the universe and channel your thoughts about your future and find the answers to accomplish it. You will change, and your thinking too.

To begin, you wonder, what am I going do to get out of my bubble and start the growth? The unknown will appear, and your mind will play the same old record- the same recording that has played inside you throughout your entire life. I do understand. Instead, slow down and take yourself away from the vinyl for a while. Some of our deepest fears are that we are inadequate in some way. We are afraid of the little voice that tells us we can do anything. Then we ask ourselves, do I deserve to be brilliant, talented, or wealthy? Of course, you do. You are what you think you are. That is your attraction to the external world.

Then build good thoughts about yourself. Think about the vibration inside you like the beach boys sang about, "Good, Good, Good Vibrations." When you think you are ready, turn off the television, the smartphone, the materialistic ego world in your mind, and connect with the universe. Ask the questions in your mind about what you want to be or change; what's in your heart. Remain still, and the answers will come should you practice this technique enough. Write them down. Once you start doing this and strive every day to accomplish your list, things will change. Do not get in a hurry. Through the process, stay away from the place, the who or what that causes drama in your life. This will help you grow and mature in the knowledge of yourself and the world. It all begins in your mind, then start the process to move this knowledge to your heart. When you do, the real battle begins-the struggle of the past versus the future. It will expose things about you. It will bring you into the present. It will be a painful process at first; however, new growth.

We are all afraid of something in life. For example, I am scared to leave my dead-end job. You tell yourself, I am just unable to find, or I am unqualified for a better job. Why are you limiting yourself? Learn to expand outside your comfort zone, join a networking group, or get involved in a mentor program. Keep going until you do find the job you want in your heart. Or, I love animals and want to become a veterinarian. Go volunteer at a pet shelter or animal hospital; they would like to have you. You will meet someone to get you down that path as long as you are doing the work from your heart. Study the material, and you will go to veterinarian school if you don't make up an excuse. Or, I am no good because that's what my parents told me when I was a kid. Forgive them and feel blessed that they brought you into this world. Show them love anyway. You can only change you. You are fantastic, you just must believe that. What I am getting at is to change your thought process, get off your rear, and do something as nothing is free in this world. Turn the record over and play the right side. You are your champion. When you are positive and channel your energy towards your healing and not the drama of the 3D world, you will change, and the things you seek will find you. Growing in life and moving from bubble to bubble.

To live a happier life, we must continue to leave our comfort zone or our bubble. I'm not advocating to do dangerous things or make yourself look like a fool. Some things are not in our destiny. Skydiving or being a standup comedian, for example. Life is about experiences and overcoming our fears. When we leave our comfort zone, it opens things that we would have never realized we enjoyed and experiences that we would have never incorporated into our lives. Our bubble only makes up a part of our reality, and our life's bubbles need to expand. You must burst your bubble to start to change your life and your surroundings. Traveling, for example, a great way to experience things you would have never experienced. You have experiences and lists you want to do in life, do them! Do not allow fear or reasons to stop you. Life isn't a race; it's about leaving behind the past, desires, and silly beliefs and living a life filled with fun, love, and experiences. It's about building memories with the people you love. Do what is on your bucket list before it's too late, that way you do not have any regrets.

Along the journey, talk to people you usually would not approach. People are attracted to their mirror or people like them; it's comfortable. That's why certain groups of people hang out with each other. You attract what you think of yourself, and you are your surroundings. However, how in the world do we know whether we have something in common with someone unless we talk with them? Interacting with others outside our bubble exposes us to a different view of the world, which may be a more beautiful reality. Life only ends when you allow it to, instead, live your entire life, every single minute, hour and day. Get busy living, not dying. Start living before you find out you have a health or some crisis that you think is going to end your life. Bust your bubble every day. Once you bust your bubble and the more things you cross off your list, the more you add to your life and life story. You will not live forever, at least your flesh; however, your soul is another story.

Jumping from bubble to bubble in life takes courage. A conscious thought process is telling yourself that you need to keep experiencing life in all its glory. It's the same old internal record that keeps us from it. That's what our ego wants, to be comfortable and not face our fears. Our hearts and soul seek knowledge of our meaning and experiences. One must find additional knowledge outside their bubble to grow. These bubbles we create for ourselves are only part of our reality. The real truth is when you get out into the world and make new friends, see new places, and experience different cultures. Attempt to get out of your bubble; you are in one whether you realize it or not. By letting go of the same old thoughts of the past and fearful thoughts of the future, we open ourselves to the new energy. The courage to believe in ourselves, forgive ourselves, forgive others, and move past our fears to the growth we all seek. When you keep learning and conquer your fears, the universe will steer you in the right direction and connect you to people and places that create happiness. Pop that bubble you are in and get out there and enjoy your life. Change the record to understand that you can accomplish anything. You will be surprised by what the universe has to offer and reward you with when you do.

THE MIRROR

"Behavior is the mirror in which everyone shows their image."
– Johann Wolfgang von Goethe

Life is like a mirror, the better we think on the inside, the abundance we receive on the outside. The idea is that everything you experience is a direct reflection of your emotions, actions, and thoughts. Just think, your life reflects your inner self. You receive what you give. Should you be kind, giving, loving, you will receive the same in return. Should you be mean, negative, unforgiving, these emotions will attract those outcomes. The rule comes into play of how people treat you is their karma; how you respond is yours. People will treat you the way you treat them. Imagine that, your mind and your emotions direct or attract your life movie. Most of the obstacles in life we face are self-imposed; our minds are the cause or solution. That requires some thought, let's dive in and see where the reflection takes us.

People find it scary sometimes to look at themselves in a mirror. They do not like what they see at times. They think I'm something I do not recognize. Why? Why do we do this? It's subconscious and just how we are programmed; however, when we move past the depth of skin to within and change that, our outer world reflects those changes. As the mirror of life is a direct reflection of our reality and inner self. Most people think their problems come from outside conditions. However, our thoughts that are out of alignment with the universe attract our lessons. Life is a mirror that reflects your image; your inner feelings are the basis for human interaction.

We live in a holographic universe in a pattern that is part of a larger one. The mirror of life dictates our relationships on all levels. What? We find ourselves or our reflection through other people and our relationships with them. The outer world is a response to our inner world. You create your life with your thoughts. Everyone we interact with in life is the mirror and dictates back to us what we think about ourselves. When we understand ourselves through relationships, whether good or bad, we learn every interaction comes from our thoughts. When we are affected by other people's actions or words, we react to what we see or do not like about ourselves. "Mirror Mirror on the Wall, who is the fairest of them all?" Remember that story?

The key to the mirror is understanding the self's thoughts. To retrain our mind to become positive. To be consciously aware when we go somewhere, not focus on something that makes us complain, to be grateful for something. To run towards our fears and conquer them, not the opposite. Everything we think about in life is a direct reflection of what we feel about ourselves. We have all done stupid things, I least I have. We are not perfect, and sometimes it takes multiple encounters to learn and to forgive. It all boils down to the inner thoughts and what we are speaking to others, such as adding "karma" to a bad situation.

When some of us consume too much alcohol or a substance and make a mistake, mess up, says something, do something, we experience an emotion the next day. That would not happen in ancient Egypt at the consumption festival. Down the road, we are calm, and someone else is drunk. Doing or saying dumb things. Some of us feel anger towards them, why? Why are we angry at someone who did the same thing as possibly us? We are reflecting on the emotion we felt when we woke up the next morning and someone was upset with us. Instead, take all events as a lesson to learn and grow. To find and cure what made us do this in the first place. Some things are a constant struggle; however, anyone can overcome any issue or addiction in life by forgiving and facing their past.

When you notice the behavior of another towards others and yourself, you understand the mirror. You know the world reacts to one's thoughts of the inner self. Everyone we meet in life is directed through the universe at the right time to reflect something to us to correct something inside we are craving to fix. To guide us to self-love and self-forgiveness-to the process of owning our behavior so we can become a mirror of light to others. One is continually creating the world around them with their thoughts. Reality is the mirror of your inner world. The choices we make are the conditioned beliefs carried from our upbringing. We have no control over this; however, life offers you feedback so that you can act to correct negative self-thoughts should that be the case and heal the past.

People show all the time, you have no idea why, by saying or doing something and you wonder what the heck. When you listen to your inner self about what they are telling you, you understand yourself. Every message in life is a lesson; you just must decipher what it means. For example, I had a little girl I met at the pool. She was six. In the beginning, it was strange how she opened to me about me. Yes me. She called me T-Love. We hung out over most the summer and died down as I made her ask her mother for permission to do anything with me, like swim or sit by me, etc.… What I learned later from a friend is that this was a message that I was on the right path, that's all. You never know who will send you these messages, even a six-year-old.

Our life is to figure out love for ourselves by loving what we think we do not like about ourselves. We all have had our Judas in life. Whether you believe this or not, our Judas, the person or people who get on our nerves or sometimes hurts us the most, is sometimes our greatest teacher. Those Judas' relationships guided me to learn that my family, all my family, are the most beautiful people I have ever known and filled with love. I learned making myself happy in life is the journey. I learned to love myself and how to set boundaries. I learned that I am a seed that the universe has created to grow. I learned the soil we should all seek is one that encourages growth, love, and abundance. That action changed my outside world to love and abundance, mostly, as I still interact with people who do not think this way.

My dad always said, "Peace of mind is priceless." According to Wikipedia, "Inner peace (or peace of mind) refers to a deliberate state of psychological or spiritual calm despite the potential presence of stressors. Being "at peace" is considered by many to be healthy (homeostasis) and the opposite of being stressed or anxious. It is a state where our mind performs at an optimal level with a positive outcome. Peace of mind is thus generally associated with bliss, happiness, and contentment." Peace is not something that begins in the outside world; it starts from within. Peace is not in lousy soil; pain is. Seek the soil that grows your seed and your life.

Another example is parents and coaches; they can get on your nerves, you are upset; however, when you grow up and look back, you realize what they were teaching you. They do this because they care. A parent or a coach that doesn't ride your ass doesn't care. There is a correlation. Think about the guy or gal the coach never talks to or yells at, does he or she play a lot? Or the parents that never check homework or report cards? When people harass you, it means they care, of course, in a positive moving direction. We learn from these people by reflecting on ourselves to make ourselves better. We overcome what made us react and understand it; we heal it. When we use love to solve these challenges, these very people see it and behave differently, like your coach freaking out because your team won the championship or your parents crying when you graduate from high school or college. It's the mirror that reflects these behavior growths and the universe guiding you.

On a positive note, the desirable behaviors we see in others are also reflections of ourselves—qualities of caring, loving, altruism, respect, and trust. When we project these qualities to others, it forces them to look inside themselves to determine their real attributes. It's natural and subconscious. When they react to us and are upset, they are angry at themselves for not displaying these traits. That's how it works. Over time, they may learn from these experiences, and they may not, they are the ones that determine that outcome. When displayed to others over time, these traits can become contagious and change a whole family, social group, neighborhood, or geographical area. My entire volleyball league changed, and now we are a tight-knit group of people who care for one another. Amazing!

When we choose thoughts of love, we live in a world of passion. In other words, as we focus on making ourselves better, we bring out the best within others. Do not shy away from the mirror as sometimes your greatest enemy is your most prominent teacher. When you learn how the mirror works with others, you began not only to understand them; you began to understand yourself. Keep putting good thoughts out into the universe and pay attention to people. They can teach you a lot about yourself. Learn from every mirror you meet in your life. You may become someone's biggest mirror, the most excellent teacher in their life, what a privilege. Imagine that!

THE LITTLE BOX

"The curious idea that your genitals dictate your behavior."
– Merlyn Gabriel Miller, *Sex, Death, Drugs & Madness*

It's interesting when you step back from the world as an observer; you conclude that every creature on the planet over a certain age thinks with their genitals. It's everywhere you go, I mean to an extent, work, gatherings, in the sky, nature, everywhere. It's like air. Some creature is chasing another and thinking something. I mean, hey, that's the way it's been since the beginning of time; otherwise, there would be no more creatures. We are programmed that way, all beings, both sexes, do this stuff. With humans, it's a little different, however, the same as nature. My buddy always says, should you not be thinking about sex, your mind is wandering. It's funny and a joke, of course, however, very factual. The desires of the flesh create most of the emotional trouble in our human lives. That desire leads people to become jealous, angry, enemies, envious, immoral, divide, argue, and live by their ego. However, when you move past that thought stream and live by the spirit of your soul, it leads you to love, joy, peace, patience, kindness, goodness, humility, and self-control. It leads you to freedom and inner happiness. It leads you to the people and places to figure out the love of yourself, others, and your meaning.

We have all been in relationships, well, most of us. We find someone, and we are overwhelmed with them. We feel something inside for them. We are attracted to them in many ways, especially sexually. Come on. Then we begin spending time together. We date for a while or even get married. Eventually, the blind love wears off, and the true self appears—the one who lives deep inside all of us. Then we must face the reality of whether it's love at all. It surrounds us everywhere.

I talked with a man at the bar I frequented one Friday evening when I did not have any plans or a date. He sat down around seven-fifteen PM and gave me some look like, hey, I do not go out much and want to talk. This kind of stuff happens to me now since my journey began as my aura seems to illuminate. I know what you're thinking, it's not visible. I started talking and laughing with him about all kinds of stuff in about ten minutes. We had more drinks, and the guy just opened it to me. He had been married for eighteen years and had two children that were sixteen and fourteen, I think. The talk quickly turned into discussing his wife. He said, "Women evolve differently than men; I'm the same; she is nowhere near the woman I married." I said, huh, internally. I told him that men are boys, a lot of us grow older, just not up. I have no idea why, that's just the way we are; period. Women, most women, grow up and continue to evolve (this is a trait more men need to recognize and start doing in their lives) and are smarter about love and relationships. Most women are light years ahead of men on this stuff. Women run the world. And you thought it was money and power, well, what do wealth and power buy you? And should a woman understand this, they can use men's desires to get what their heart desires from men who do not pay attention to the relationship's foundation. Beyond the physical, the beauty of the most beautiful creature, the universe created, the female species. It's the overall attraction by all when grace is present. The best way I can explain is when a beautiful woman walks into a restaurant or arrives at a pool, everybody, even women, stop and look. It's just the way it is and the way it has always been. Males just take it a step further. Wait, what is the little box? The Holy Grail? It's part of the female species, use your imagination.

You know everything a man does from the time he's in sixth grade is for women. What? Think about it. Men get in shape, play sports, join the band, join the choir, get an education, well some men, get a job, and make money. Why? Why do we torture ourselves? For women, we want women or a woman. However, we run into trouble attracting the right woman. Many men go for looks and not inner beauty. We start going out with a woman and know nothing about her background or history. We have a beautiful woman at our side, who cares. We all wind up is some situation and cannot figure it out. In some cases, there is no logical solution, and some women do the same thing with men. Everything about a relationship boils down to yours and their background, desires, history, childhood, and subconscious. Important stuff. Very!!!

Most males are born with certain traits, jealousy and lust are big ones, and programmed, for one thing, procreation. Many men release stress through sex. Men need sex for several reasons, mainly their confidence and to pass on their genes. Observe a whitetail buck in rutting season or a bull in a pasture with twenty cows. A buck or a bull will fight another to the death for a doe or a cow. Many men will do the same. We're all the same to some extent. What makes human men different is we have some mental capacity to control it, most do. However, you would not believe that as of late with all the hashtag movements. I admit that men's minds wander these days due to the dress code that has changed in society, yoga pants everywhere.

Back to the story, the guy said all kinds of things about his wife. However, he never said he loved her. He told me this and that, and then I asked, have you ever taken her on vacation or dinner to just talk and not tried anything sexual? Sirens. I mean a look of someone lost in the mountains of Colorado or Oregon or somewhere. He didn't realize that his actions, gestures, and everything he strived for were based on desire and not love. We ended the conversation, and I never saw the guy again; however, when he left that night, he said, "Thank you, I am going to give it a shot." Who knows what he did or what happened, hopefully, he put himself back on a path of love? Just like you can.

After reflecting on some of my relationships, I saw myself in this guy. It's the bubble you get into in relationships, sometimes. Instead of enjoying the moment and creating memories, I was chasing the desires. Many men zoom past the romance and companionship that women crave and move right to the sex. Everything requires a foundation, especially romantic relationships. Imagine building a house or any structure with no foundation, it's impossible. You must create the foundation for it to be successful; unless one only wants to satisfy their desires. However, today there are so many issues men and women deal with from their past. Society, in general, that affect how this is interpreted and misconstrued daily all over the world. You must recognize the behavior of desires, both men and women, and consciously fix it together. You must work on the foundation. You do this by talking. Talking about your relationship with each other leads to building trust, so when you go out into the world together, there is no drama, jealousy, or trouble; there is love and memories. Be on the same page and be honest with each other. Eliminate any issues that create a problem or recognize them and say good-bye. You see, I never realized that women view men as a burden, and I never realized men view women as a sex box, I wasn't paying attention.

It's a revelation when you step back from the world and the amount of sex that surrounds us on TV, movies, at bars, at beaches, in politics, at work, you name it. It's tough not to buy in when society, politicians, entertainers, athletes, and movies remove the blueprint and teachings of the universe from everything they say and do; definition of secular. What is the vacuum? It's what you see and hear on the news, what you see in society, politics, and hear about from your friends and families.

Significant dysfunction, evil, power, and greed. Make yourself aware and to not buy into this way of life. That's not life. The real meaning of life is about being happy, doing the right thing, forgiving others, helping others, loving people, and changing people's lives for the better.

Many things used to be sacred; now, they are just mainstream. Both men and women need to look at their relationships and the foundation. Men are boys in big boy pants, cars, trucks, and houses. We do dumb things that keep us entertained; women meet up with their friends for lunch or dinner. They talk about this stuff; men do not. In my opinion, men need to evolve, keep evolving, get off the damn couch, and chat with other men. Men need to do some yoga or go running or fly out to some beach with their woman for two or three days and get away from the same old same old. Some men, however, do not look at it this way, and they chase their desires. Some not, and some abuse their social and wealth power to get what they want. Some women exploit men's eagerness to get what they want, and some use it to build their control over men or their man. That is why so many men and women are walking around like zombies and upset with their love life. Drinking, doing drugs, angry, depressed, it's all over the place. Take the time to step back and determine what your relationship is with each other. Find the security and trust with each other before something happens or construed happened. No one should allow desires to control the happiness of the relationship. That should be by sacrificing yourselves to a higher power, growing together, and let's say it together, using love.

When you remove yourself from the 3D world of desires of the flesh, the emotion of love for people becomes the focus. When using love instead of lust, there is a different experience, a high, a euphoria, and should it be mutual a beautiful union. It brings you closer and creates lasting love should you recognize it. When you discuss things together, you can move past so much that destroys relationships today. Just be honest with each other. Instead of all the negative energy, build the memories filled with love and fun, not the crazy love, drama games. Your energy focuses on making your lives and future together. Your frequencies will evolve together, and you will be closer on all levels of your relationship. Shit, you may even buck the trend and live together until one of you dies. Therefore, you sometimes hear about a couple that has been married for a long time, dies minutes or days apart. Unique stuff right there. A real connection and an understanding of love between a man and a woman. Two soul mates with the balance of love, trust, and the truth of life completed by the other. The full circle of life. Imagine living with someone who understands the dynamics, love, and that life is about fun, not games. Get over the desires, and you get over half of life's struggles. Conquer them, do not let them conquer you and your thoughts! There are only two people that can do this, that's the two of you!

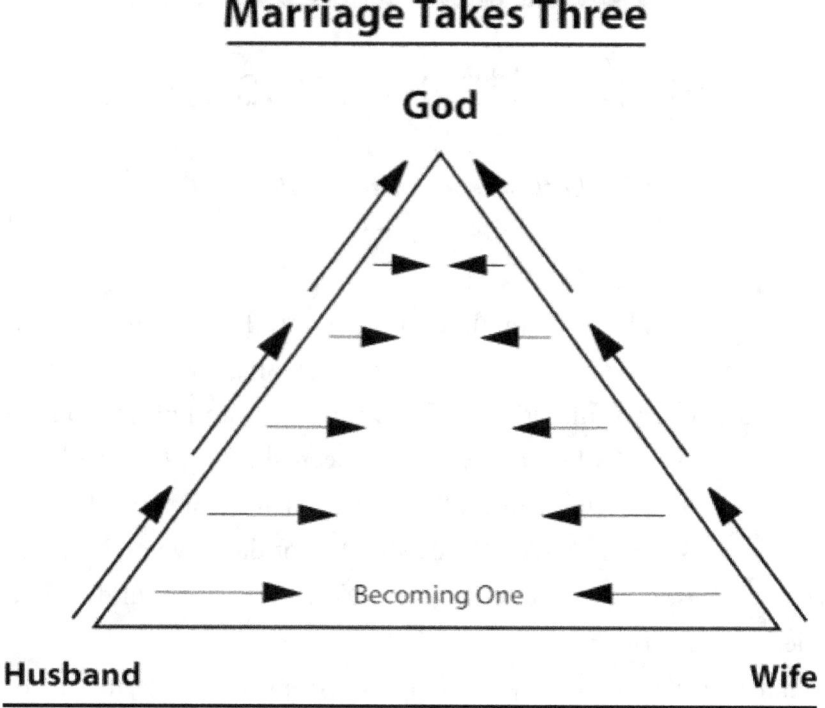

The closer the two of you get to the unconditional love, the closer you get.

BROKEN HEART SYNDROME

"The hottest love has the coldest end."
– Socrates

So, you have made it through to this point. I bet you are thinking differently about your life and the people you share your life experience with. I finally learned many songs, books, movies, and plays; you name it is a result of a broken heart. Yes, I have been sleeping!!! A broken heart is just a learning mechanism and a path to a new place. Life is tough, however, very short. A broken heart should not destroy your joy and life. There is a lesson to a broken heart. Your job is to understand the experience and grow from it.

What a revelation what you can learn from heartbreak, no one breaks your heart, only you do with false expectations. Love comes from within, not from others, and only permeates through you to others. Our understanding that our value or worthiness is what we think about ourselves and the healthy relationships we participate in can create a path to find loving relationships. We are all put on this planet to learn a lesson from the past and correct it in this lifetime, or as I have stated, it will repeat until we do. Therefore, we should strive daily to find our true self, our correct path, and the true love for ourselves.

We all have a choice every day to live life right, be happy, think happy thoughts, and do the right thing. When we set ourselves up for unrealistic expectations in our lives, we are disappointed with the other person or the experience. We should instead be dissatisfied with ourselves. That's why it's essential to live in reality, and in the present. Not some preconceived ideas we may have. We all do this with all kinds of situations; however, with love, it hurts the most. It also depends on what side of the broken heart you are on. That can be a lesson too. As the saying goes, just because you can do something to somebody, doesn't mean you should. So be truthful with people, they may not like it or accept it, however, they will respect it and you eventually. And sometimes, you do not realize what you got until it's gone. The biggest quest is to be truthful with yourself.

Most of us have had a broken heart at some point in our life and struggled for a while. When we learn to let go of relationship struggles of the past, alleviate the pain and negative energy that causes, we can focus on moving our lives forward. Life is short and creating healthy relationships that build love and happiness is the key to inner happiness. It's imperative to know where we stand in our relationships. To determine how healthy and whether we are growing or living in pain. When heartbreak happens, it takes time to allow our hurt ego to die, build ourselves back up, and learn from it. We have then hopefully learned to forgive ourselves and others as we are not perfect, and neither are they. When we are at peace within ourselves, the real favors of life appear. You will be fine and will heal over time, trust me.

Love is mysterious and can overpower logic. We just love some people no matter what, and that sometimes is a sign that we need some form of healing. What most of us do not understand is heartbreak is a blessing in disguise and is the universe guiding us to heal within. The setbacks and mistakes set us up to do something amazing once we let go, learn the lesson and put the light of love back in our hearts. As they say, no pain, no gain. When you recognize that and do not allow the situation to go the other way in anger or despair, you learn about yourself. We are like the bush that requires pruning, sometimes we are in a period of growth, and everything seems to be going our way, and sometimes we need to be cutback to grow again. A heartbreak is us learning future relationship growth.

Life, relationships, and love are not fair sometimes; nobody ever said life is fair, that is a false expectation we set up for ourselves. The setbacks, struggles, and heartache are just part of the journey to our destiny. When you trust your intuition and follow the little voice inside, you do not find yourself in a bad relationship. You'll recognize it and end it with grace should you be spiritually mature. You know what peace is, and you do not participate in activities that cause hurt and guilt anymore. When you put your love out there and are responsible for all your actions in all its forms, you allow yourself to find a relationship that is full of growth. Love wants to build the character of the person who stands before them.

When you step back, out of the bubble, realize your weaknesses, the real understanding arises. We understand why we allow others to hurt us and the knowledge to see it and overcome it. We know our insecurities, and we heal them. We learn not to act on emotions and not to take everything personally. We learn to set the correct relationship boundaries and expectations, so we do not give our power and feed self-love-the inner emotional healing to self-improvement. You learn a relationship is about building each other up, not destroying each other. That is the pure love of yourself that can move on, forgive others, forgive ourselves, learn to stand up for ourselves, let go, and be happy without all the relationship drama involved. That leads us to discover a reciprocal loving partner.

Robust relationships teach, not hurt you. Fighting for relationships you know is never going to work will drain you. The ego can create incredible drama in relationships. You must communicate with that person whether you are even in a relationship to understand your place, time, emotions, type of relationship you are in, and where the relationship is going. Some of us do not do this; we assume things and live in wonderment or fear of what to do next. We all need to figure out what the relationship foundation is before we make the emotional attachment. To know where the relationship goals and future lie. Life is full of these experiences.

When we do not have control over our emotions, we project that to others in our relationships. We lose ourselves in someone under the guise of love. We have stepped out of empowerment and into the ego madness. Through boundaries, we inherit the clarity of insight and whether a relationship is sturdy or not. We do not allow others to control our emotions and learn that emotions are responsible for the self. We learn that our happiness is determined by ourselves and not the responsibility of others.

Once we learn these lessons, we do not allow others to destroy us like so many other people. We use the pain for strength. We turn the negative energy positive. We learn by setting boundaries in relationships. We learn that love is not sex, and sex is not love. That sex is just a bonus or icing on the cake of a beautiful, healthy, loving relationship. We learn to own our emotions and create boundaries that protect us from the hurt. We learn that love frees us from the past and the future. It gives us the gift to live in the present. By letting go, forgiving them, and yourself, your positive energy will heal the wound. So, take your time and get on with your life by doing something you lost in the relationship. Plant the seed of self-love. Go for a walk, go for a run, take a trip, call your parents or siblings, hang out with old friends, and do something positive.

Thinking the correct, positive way is to look within and figure yourself out or the person you allowed to break your heart. Maybe you have issues, or perhaps they have problems. We all have issues we are dealing with; everyone has crosses to bear. We just deal with death, parents, relationships, and life differently. Learn to own your emotions and dig into yourself to figure out what is missing. We are all looking to fill in the hole. Then heal the darkness by using self-love and let it all go.

Forgive yourself and forgive them. Love is about loving someone for who they are, not changing them.

Getting over a broken heart is different for everyone; however, we all share that hurt in our chest. It's our soul telling us that we care for something other than ourselves just as much. You must love yourself before you can be loved by others. Leaving someone is severe; however, your joy and happiness is the journey. We make soul contracts with others to teach us our life lessons. Nothing shows up in our lives that don't have a reason for being, and that reason is to teach us something. All forms of love bring us an abundance of the universe. Our work is to decipher the lesson, overcome it, and make our lives better.

To love is to love yourself and not fall prey to an unhealthy relationship of any kind. Learn your lessons and embrace the love you want for your life. A link takes two, don't fight it too long, you will lose yourself. You must sometimes let who you love go, and should they love you, they may come back. Then forgive them, no matter how hard that is, and set new boundaries. The rest is up to them.

Your heart is more than a pump; it's a gateway to your soul. Being heartbroken is a tough ride; however, should you handle it properly (heal it) by staying away from substances, give yourself some alone time and don't jump into bed with whatever is walking, you will learn and grow from it. A broken heart is a tool to use and a path for future relationships. Learn to settle all the wounds.

The most significant relief is that you are not in that heart-wrenching relationship anymore. Staying around will only make you miserable. Sitting home alone will not help. Go out and have some damn fun and get your mind off it. Find an outlet so that you can release the attachment. Build something, read something, write something, or learn something new. Listen to the universe and your inner voice for the messages. End the practice of following the desires of the flesh and getting your heart broke because you want someone to love you. It will happen as long as you love yourself and stay on your path. When you love yourself, and just be yourself, love will find you. Address the real issues, yours or theirs, and understand that should it have been meant to be, it would have been, it's that simple. Maybe it was just the wrong time. That's how the universe works and is guiding you.

A large part of our society is experiencing a broken heart or a broken relationship. Have a conversation with friends, co-workers, or your family members. It's due to the family's breakdown and that most people are separated from the love of the universe. It's the present thought that the external world full of desires and worldly possessions make you happy when really, it's the inner world that does. Search within and change your thoughts to understand love and watch your world change. It means that you do not have to experience a broken heart with the correct understanding that a relationship with a foundation, boundaries, and proper expectations is the answer. Take the positive things out of every relationship. Then do something positive and productive with that energy. You can achieve anything in your life when you channel your energy.

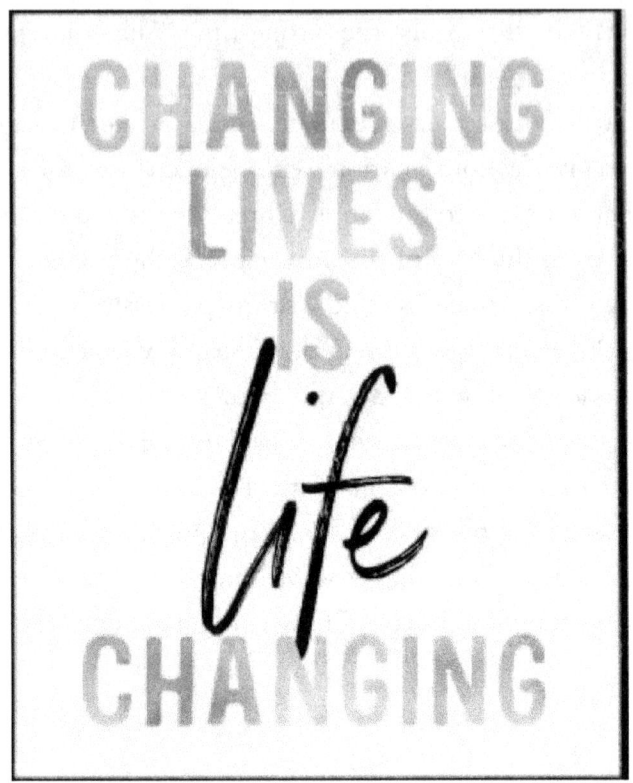

CHANGING THE LIVES OF OTHERS

*"Regardless of whatever I do, I know what my purpose is:
to make a difference in people's lives."*
– Tim Tebow

I consider this section one of the most important traits we can acquire in our lifetime, change someone, for good. Changing other's people's lives is all about learning our lessons and growing from what we perceive we have done wrong, wrongs towards us, letting the love of the universe into our heart, and giving back to people. By learning the lessons and passing them on to others, we change lives, especially for younger people. When we help others, we are promoting or healing ourselves. That's what life is all about, improving our self, being happy, helping others, love, people, and the love of people. Let's explore this.

I was two-hundred, and sixty-nine pounds slept in late, ate fast food, didn't exercise, and drank alcohol more than I should have. I had high cholesterol and high blood pressure. I was happy, I thought. However, one day at the pool, there was this girl that I found attractive, and a younger guy left at the end of the evening. She liked both of us, however, decided that the younger, in shape guy, was her man. I wasn't hurt or anything; it just made me think. And in the end, I was blessed, and so were they as she did go with him. They got married, had a son, and so on. What that did for me was again to start reflecting on myself. That thought changed how I thought about myself and others. I began to change my life and, in return, began to give back in all situations and change others' lives. Why? I realized life is not about me; it's way more prominent; it's about others and allowing the flow of the universe to work without blaming something-the part of me that saw empathy in everything and everyone.

A friend of mine was a real workout junky. She encouraged me to get back to the gym, which I enjoyed as I was a baseball pitcher in college and used to run and work out. One day she challenged me on social media to start doing twenty-two pushups a day for the twenty-two veterans who commit suicide every day. I'm a patriot and began doing pushups; I started posting them on social media. I did this for thirty days straight. People started noticing and sending me notices and all kinds of stuff. Anyway, this went on for weeks, and I ended the project. I did not think much of it.

About three months later, I was at this party in San Antonio, Texas, my old hometown, and this dude came up to me and said, "Hey T-Bone," my nickname, "You changed my life?" I said, "What?" He said, "Those pushups you were doing, I couldn't do more five pushups, however, when I saw you, I kept going and now can do twenty-five at a time. I am doing more active things and have lost ten pounds." I said, wow, internally, and we talked about it for a while and then about his family. It was a fun time. After everyone had left the party, I thought about how it made me feel that I changed someone else's life by doing pushups. I felt good about myself and him. That action spurred me to actively, when asked, help others in their life. Later down the road, three other people told me the same thing about the pushups. What I am saying is that little things can change people's lives.

As I stated before, I go out, and people just start talking with me. Even when I go to the grocery store, I end up talking with people. I was at the bar one evening, imagine that, and I rolled up and this young man, Matt, worked there. I said, Matthew, how are you, Luke, John, and Paul doing this evening? The guy sitting to my right turned to me as he had just seen a miracle. We began to chat and had a few drinks. He then told me how he had been to drug rehab nine times and had a large family with issues.

Over an hour or so, he received a few text messages and was all upset. I said "What's up;" he said it was his sister, and she needed money. He said, screw her and went into how they fight, and he doesn't go over much or join the family because it's always a big fight. I said, have you tried using love? He said, what? I said, "Instead of using anger, let's say it together, use love." I said, "Send her a text and tell her you can get it tomorrow, and I love you." He reluctantly did, took him about five minutes, and I saw the wheels turning. About three minutes later, his sister replied with a message: "That would be fine, I love you too, and we should get together more often." He was stunned. We talked for an hour so more while watching a game on the TV, he said thank you, hugged me and left. About three weeks later, he saw me again and said, "you changed my life, dude." I used to love now with my family, and it has turned completely around. We are getting along great. Thank you. Love again!

One day at the pool, an older woman and her daughter was in a wheelchair. They were strolling around and seemed lost. Nobody paid attention to them, so I went over and said, would you like to sit at my table? The look! Well, they sat down, and we chatted for a while. I didn't think much about it. The next time I was down there, they would show up, and we would visit. I would give them a beer, and we would listen to music on my Bluetooth speaker. One day I stopped by over at their place, and we started chatting. I began stopping by almost every day after the gym to check on them.

At the time, I was going through some relationship stuff and wanted their advice since they are women. We not only discussed that, but we also dove into all sorts of discussions about religions, politics, men, life; you name it. She was a poet, and we started reading her work, and she played some type of instrument, a small harp of some sort and singing songs. I ended up meeting their entire extended family. Later, we discussed some of the relationships of their family. I suggested a few things, using love and honesty mostly, and never asked again. A few weeks later, she said I helped in fixing the relationship of their whole family. She expanded to say that since our friendship and all the discussions we had, I changed their lives and their entire family's life. They were happier, and their whole family was also. They viewed life differently now and wanted to live more, even though it was hard. I was very appreciative and proud that I could help in any way. I also conveyed to them that they changed my life at the same time by demonstrating love, friendship, and overall acceptance of me and who I was and becoming. They helped me understand my struggles, first-world issues, and overcoming them. When you help others, it ends up healing you. The mirror is a powerful thing in life.

Once you understand the unconditional love from the universe and live this way, you will recognize how blessed you are. You will be put into situations to help others. Understand and accept that. Along the way, many of us lose track. Some of us let the external world and people to run their emotions and thoughts. Some just do not understand what they do to themselves as their ego blinds them.

One day I arrived home from work, and a car inside the gate was blocking the entrance to the parking lot. I thought, wow, there is no damage or smoke. It was a Cadillac with paper license plates with the door slightly open. There was water running below the vehicle from the A/C, so I knew it had been there awhile. I felt nervous as though someone was in some medical condition. I squeezed by and saw a young lady sitting in the car very disheveled. I parked in a parking spot and walked up to the vehicle, waving cars by, as everyone else squeezed by also, upset and went on. I came up to the window and the young lady, scantily dressed, crying, on the phone with a lit cigarette in her hand, half-drunk or more.

I said, "Are you okay?" she didn't answer, I repeated it, and she said, "Are you a cop," twice. I said no, "I live here, and I'm concerned for you." She was surprised; however, her attitude changed. She couldn't figure out her new, used car, so I got in, asked her permission, moved it out of the way to a parking spot, and said, "Would you like to talk?" Oh boy, Pandora's Box, minus the hope and minus love, know the story? I will not repeat much; however, she was a lost soul in life, been to jail for a DWI, got beat up there, and lost two teeth. She was being beaten by her boyfriend, who went to prison for doing it only to have her bail him out. Wow, huh? I spoke to her for over ten minutes and explained that she didn't respect and love herself, I asked, and she said, "I do not love myself."

I went on to say that to find herself and love herself that she needed to get rid of this guy, the rocks and weeds in her garden, and understand that loving someone who cheats, beats, and uses you is no way to live. She then said, "I have a broken heart." I said "We all had had one; you cannot let it destroy you. You allow it to put you on another path." We went back and forth with this and a bunch of intimate details that I reflected her to show the self-destruction. She understood, and I left as her "boyfriend" was looking for her.

The message here is to be a healer, not a judge with broken people. Do your best to help people as the higher power hung with you when you did something wrong, like me? Once you connect and understand unconditional love, opportunities to help people with arise. Help them. Everybody must promote themselves in the end. Be their mirror, be their teacher, and be their healer.

Little things can change someone else's life. Doing pushups, just saying hello in a public place, listening, putting yourself in someone else's shoes, paying attention to what's going on in their lives, or simply having a relationship with a custodian at school for a young person. Helping and demonstrating love can change their day and possibly their life. By contributing, you elevate your vibration; you will attract people who need help. Help them as you are helping and healing yourself! Open your mind and use kindness when you are in these situations. Your life is about you; however, also about others. Empathy is a strong trait that conveys great internal love, and when used correctly, can make a massive difference in the lives of others. It only takes one person to change someone's life, and maybe that can be you. When you care about others, your whole self illuminates. People sense the energy. Changing other people's lives will, in turn, change your life for the better.

BE YOURSELF

"Be yourself; everyone else is already taken."
– Terence Shannon

I have fifty-three first cousins and twenty aunts and uncles. These folks are the most fabulous people I have ever met. I am pretty much the youngest of them all and have never had an issue with any of them. I am surrounded by love when I am with them. It's a real blessing that I have come to realize over time. I have been asleep to some blessings in my life. I will focus this section on my dad's brother; we'll just call him uncle. And man, this guy has always been something. Amazing.

My uncle is about five-feet-eight or nine inches tall, seventy-seven years old, grey hair, small build, and about one hundred and fifty pounds. He has three kids; two have moved away to other states, and one lives about thirty miles away. He has this reputation of being an old crab or getting people upset and so on. He just likes to harass folks, in my opinion. Well, I never had much of an issue with the guy. To be honest, I don't think I knew the man or even attempted to. He moved to the Texas Coast about eighteen years ago. He fishes every day possible, except when the weather is bad or on weekends when all hell breaks loose around the boat ramps. I love fishing, so I decided a few years ago to stay at his place. I called him up and asked, "Hey, big guy, may I come down for a week, stay at your place, and go fishing with you?" He said sure; "There are rules though," I said "Okay." I rolled down there and went over the rules and stayed out of the guy's way. Over a few days, things seem to smooth out. We had good days catching fish and so on. A couple of days where windy, so I worked out, drove around, messed around, ate seafood, and hung at this bar. Imagine that.

One morning we were out on the bay on his boat. Very early, the sun coming up, orange sky, orange water reflecting the sun's rays, mullet jumping, birds wading, dolphins surfacing, and name it. We pulled up to this spot and began to get ready to wade fish. We grabbed our nets, stringers, poles, tackle, etc. He said, man, you lost fifty pounds, what the hell happened to you? I said I let it all go and released all my demons, mainly your nephew, my brother, who had died twenty-seven years ago. I realized that I should not park my life there, he would not want me to destroy myself and be happy in life. He said, "Wow," and became a little distant. I said, let me ask you something, he said, "Okay." I said, "It seems that you are a lot happier now, are you?" He said "Yes." I said, "What was it?" He said "It's that convent down the street where I give all my fish to the nuns and pray every day." I said, "What is it about that place in particular?" He said, "I do not know; I'm just happier now than ever." And that was it.

About four months later, Hurricane Harvey was churning in the Gulf of Mexico. I was to go down to the coast on Labor Day weekend. The storm gained strength, and I began to wonder where it would make landfall. My dad called me, and we discussed the trip and the hurricane. He said "It would be fine." A day or two later, we talked again, and I said, "There is no way I am going to be able to go; this thing is incredible and headed straight for Rockport, Texas." He then said, "I think you're right" after some discussion, he mentioned that the storm is probably going to destroy my uncle's house. I had a thought, and this feeling came over me that his home would make it somehow. Much like a verse that states "Believe, believe in the love and the higher power, live your life that way, and you will be protected from disease, harm, and death by day and night." This thing hit with one-hundred and twenty-seven miles per hour winds; the eye was a mile south of him. After the storm, my uncle's house was one of a very few in the area that was spared. He was able to move back in three weeks and have some repairs done within three months. He just had to repair a few windows, some floor tiles, siding, and his roof. He was the only one in his cull-d-sac and a large geographical area that moved back into his home. I received pictures from his son, my cousin, that displayed a war zone, destroyed homes, debris everywhere, no streetlights, and uprooted trees. Why was his house saved? Because he is a fisherman and gives his catch to the nuns and prays with them every day? Well, you decide. I believe I know, back to the story. He slid off the boat and went on his way to the other side of the reef. I sat there in the glory of the morning and realized two things about my uncle, he opened to me for the first time, though slightly, and he found happiness at age seventy-five. Yes, age seventy-five.

We find ourselves thinking what our purpose is and what makes us happy at a certain point in life. We wonder what this life all about, or some of us never think of it. Like the sayings, fat and happy or ignorance is bliss. Once you cross over the preverbal lines of enlightenment, you can never go back to the ignorance part. The process leads one to find their meaning and let go of the dysfunction in themselves, the world, and people. Spirituality presents opportunities to grow and distance yourself from all the negative drama. My uncle never changed; he didn't need to; it was the rest of us who did. He found what makes him happy by being himself. He showed his true colors, like a rainbow. It took him seventy-five years. However, he did it. And so, can you. You must step back and manifest your dreams and follow them. You be you. Do not pretend to be something or somebody you are not. Be genuine, be yourself, and find your true self.

When you attempt to mimic others, we stop the universe, granting us favors for being ourselves. When we are ourselves, we attract what we want our life to be, not what others want theirs to be. When we mimic some rock star, or rap artist, or some other fad rolling around the internet, you are not yourself. Attempt to act the same anywhere you go all the time. Stay polished and be yourself through and through with your conscious self and what you believe. There is nobody on this earth like you, embrace that. As the saying goes, be yourself, everyone else is taken. By being you always with loving thoughts of yourself, your vibration will rise. People will see that you are a genuine person with a character that emits the same light in all sockets of society. By being yourself, you stand out, and your unique qualities connect you with the universe. And when you are true to yourself, your dreams in life come true.

SOCIAL MEDIA

"The more social media we have, the more we think we're connecting, yet we are disconnecting from each other."
– JR

This is a short section I think is evolving for all of us. Where to begin on this. We all know social media sites, and most of us have an account. I do, and most businesses also do. I used to hit the sites every day and post something political or about "How great my life is" and send it out. I would receive praise or start some form of argument. It was fun for a while; however, I began to fade away from the sites' personal side slowly. I began to realize that social media was a facade and influencing my attitude or happiness. For example, should I be at work and someone else was jetting off for a ski trip, I became somewhat jealous. It didn't ruin my day; I just felt something. I then began to realize that everyone was doing this, and that social media was affecting everyone's life.

Through thought, I realized social media was a facade. Most of the time, it was hiding people's real lives. It was a mask covering the true inner self. Sure, there are things people like to show off, their family, their vacations, their bodies, I could keep going. Much of social media, however, is toxic soup. I remember a friend told me about a couple he knew. Every picture on social media was something happy, parties, restaurants, kids, events, and vacations. Everyone is smiling and having fun. However, suddenly, they were getting a divorce. The real story was way different than their social media had portrayed. They even kept posting these pictures while proceeding through the divorce. A false narrative feeding the ego of perception to others. That maybe you and it may not. Social media is not where you find happiness; happiness lives inside you. We all have it. We must decipher the external messages and not allow them to direct our emotional life.

Look around the next time you are in a public place; you will see people walking around like zombies and staring at their phones. Capturing something and posting. I am not saying this is a bad thing; I suppose it's changing society. I don't mind change; however, I see the effect on folks' moral and communication skills. You have people download an app and post pictures and watch videos, cool. What I'm getting at is, should social media be making you depressed or affecting you in any way, do what I did, GET OFF!!! Put your phone down and enjoy the real world. Live your real-life and share it with your loved ones. Your life is way more important than some celebrity or an old flame's. Stop living through someone else and live through yourself. Everything in your life is not that important that you must air all your dirty laundry. You will never find your destiny should you live through others. You are the director of your life movie. Direct wisely.

FRIENDSHIP

*"It is one of the blessings of old friends
that you can afford to be stupid with them."*
– Ralph Waldo Emerson

Oh, friends. We have all had great friends and terrible friends. Friends are an essential component of our happiness. Friends of all kinds shape us, and we develop them. However, what is friendship? What makes someone a friend? I struggled with this throughout my life. And maybe you have also. A friend is someone you can trust, trust in their character, count on, talk to about anything, and are comfortable around. Someone who will help you, forgive you, love you, confide in you, and keep everything to themselves. They will keep secrets. They will help you through all the rough times and come to you for the same. They will have your back through thick and thin and will not judge you most of the time as sometimes; people make mistakes. Friends make you grow, not tear you down. That's what a friend is, period. A friend is a love. Let's dive in and determine what friendship is all about.

Friendships are for a season. Everything is beautiful for a time, and everything has a season. My first best friend was very honoree, and his parents treated me strangely. I felt I'm unsure why however believe it was because I was so different from him in so many ways. I played sports and had many friends; he was an introvert and had no friends. I think that's why I was seven. One day he called my house and asked me to go to the zoo. I called my mom at work and got it all approved. I ran over to his house, knocked on the door, and said, "Here I am, let's go, with a huge smile." His mom said you're not going, closed the door on me, and there it was-friendship over. I walked home, sad; however, I played with some kids in the neighborhood and forgot the whole thing. I am saying this may have had some effect on me and how I view friendship.

Let's jump to middle school; I had a ton of friends and had a great time. There were ups and downs and friendship changes; however, many bonds formed. You're thirteen to fifteen years old. I still communicate with some of these people. They were beautiful people, most of them, and very successful in many ways. Some days I wish I could go back to middle school for a few days and understand how lucky I was to have such a great school with so many beautiful people. Move on, and my middle school was divided up. Half went to one high school, and a half went to another. I went to a high school that was farther away from my neighborhood. I played football and baseball and met a ton of new folks.

I felt as though I never fit in with the "in" crowd in high school. Why was that? I still do not know. I mostly hung out with a few guys from my neighborhood and my older brother and his friends; however, not many people from high school. I still do not know why. I'm not upset or anything, I'm just puzzled why I didn't have more lifelong friends from high school like my eldest brother. He has a ton of friends from high school. Maybe it was a change of the times or just our class or me; I have no idea. It all shook out in the end as I moved to Austin, Texas, to play college baseball. I played ball for four years and again did not talk to a soul from the team or college. Why is that? I do not know. I see a few of them here and there as I work for a large technology company. What I am getting at is the perception that we perceive as friends may not be friends, or better, they may be.

Who you choose to be around you, that's what you are, that's your garden. Should your garden not be tended and full of rocks and weeds, you will be a rock or a weed. Your seed, your soul, your life will never grow. You must search for friends and find the fertile soil that promotes growth and encouragement. Sometimes you have what you perceive as a friend, such as when my best friend at the time ran off with my perceived girlfriend. You should then step back, think, and learn from these experiences. Pay attention to your "friends" actions to determine whether they are a true friend or an acquaintance. Remember that a true friend will love you, not romantically, no matter what. And should your best friend also be your lover, then Voila, you have hit the jackpot. Voila has a curious spelling and usually misspelled as wallah, and now you know.

Surrounding yourself with good friends and feeding off the positive advances in your lives raises your vibrations, and as you grow closer, builds up the happiness in your life. You help each other grow. Having honest friends is very important, they are blatantly honest and tell you the truth, whether you want to hear it. You learn from these things; you grow and mature should you understand and are wise enough. Listen to a true friend! The love you create with your friends makes you happy, and that happiness drives you in a positive direction. You stay high and connected to the universe and all its glory. Find good friends; they are essential to your health and well-being, not to mention someone to bounce your issues and ideas off. Bad friends will do the opposite and drain you. Having great friends is a blessing today, covet them. Be the friend you want your friends to be. Be a friend to society. Tell your friends how much you love them and show love as much as possible. True friendship is one of the highest forms of connecting to the universe. Do not waste a good bond for selfish or sensual reasons. What you receive from a true friendship is priceless. Treat it that way.

PARENTING

*"It is easier to build strong children
than to repair broken men and women."*
– Frederick Douglass

The struggle was real for my parents as they worked many hours; however, they always showed love, support, and discipline. I had a soft spot even as a child for them as we were a middle-class family, and money was tight. I have always felt such empathy for my folks—even today. I used to experience sorrow, especially for my mother, as she worked as a schoolteacher all day, then came home, made dinner, cleaned the kitchen and graded papers. She would stay up late and rise early. My father was a hard worker and left very early every morning also. For many, many years. They were always going to the grocery store or taking me to practice or games or somewhere. Even at a young age, I chipped in. I would help my mom around the house, and in return, I learned how to wash clothes, cook, bake, vacuum, dust, sew, iron, and on and on. My father taught me how to be respectful, hunt, fish, yard work, building trades, cut firewood, paint, and many other things. These are the traits my parents taught me. It was tough on them; however, they have my brother and me now to take care of them.

Being a parent is not a burden; it's a privilege. A child is a gift from the universe. It's like opening your favorite present on Christmas morning when a child is born. Open to that idea and recognize that. Having great parents that nourish, encourage, teach, and show love are the building blocks of a healthy person. Every parent is the most important thing for a child. As a parent, you teach a child's subconscious the first six to eight years of life, and that is their subconscious for their entire life. And their lies the issue with our world today. A surprising number of parents do not want to be parents. They are caught up in the hype of the day, social media, vanity, mundane things, and want to party. They do not stick it out with their mate or had a child for all the wrong reasons. They had a relationship to feel loved by someone who didn't love them. Then they search for love elsewhere, and they are missing out on the most significant blessing they will ever receive. However, in the end, you as a parent are the ones to create a kind, loving, respectable child, not the school system, not the government; you!!! Never blame others for your child's failures; it's the person you see in the mirror every morning. Think about a puppy, you must teach that dog, not that I am comparing a human to a dog here, everything—obedience, respect, manners, love, bathroom skills, basically all your knowledge. Take the time to be the best parent you can. Always be there for your child emotionally, physically, and mentally. Your child reflects you.

Whether you believe this or not, kids crave discipline. They will fight you on it; however, later, they will love you for it. I am not saying to yell at children or physically strike them, however, be firm. Yes, spank them, they need it. That is what is missing today, schools and homes is discipline. My whole neighborhood disciplined me. When I was doing something wrong, neighbors called my parents and I was punished. When I did something wrong at school, the principal called my parents and I was reprimanded at both places. That discipline teaches you how to control your emotions and become a person who takes responsibility for their actions. It teaches self-discipline and how to respect others.

Through a very tragic incident, I lost the most beautiful soul I have ever met and had a hand in molding, my son. He was handsome, funny, smart, respectful, helped others, and had many other traits. He played many sports in his short life as I did. He was a State Champion in Texas High School Football and Rugby, where he was selected to the All-State team. He is gone now; however, I was able to have him in my life for twenty-four and a half years. I have come to realize that. He is the one who bailed me out of jail when I was a fool and did not pay child support; he was eight years old. After reflecting one day, I realized, the student became the teacher. He was the one who showed me what life is about, the love of a child and a parent.

I had disciplined my son since he was very young, even though I did not see him as much as I wanted since his mother and I were divorced. I still disciplined him as though I did—nothing major as he was a phenomenal child that I will always love unconditionally. I spoke to him when for things like talking back, not saying yes and no sir, mam, not making eye contact when speaking, not doing his homework, and things I consider normal. One day, when he was in fifth-grade playing tackle football, all kinds of positions, mainly middle linebacker, I was walking along the sidelines, following the ball, just like crazy fathers do. I saw that he was moving out of plays and getting blocked every time. I yelled out to the field, he looked over, and I hand signaled him to cut into this hole to stop the run play. It worked, and he shut down that play. Another dad walks up to me and says, "I yell at my son all the time, and he never looks over, how you do that?" I will not repeat the exact words I told the guy, however in a nutshell, I said, "I disciplined the heck out of him when he was young." He looked at me with wide, owl eyes and said, "Okay," and walked off. What he did not understand is that children crave this stuff, it links their synapses in their brain for learning. You are teaching them that you care. Should there be no consequences for negative actions, who learns? Nobody!!! Discipline spurns more education and the desire to be a good upstanding citizen and display respect for all. We all want our children to be that; however, you must teach them that! My son told me that he loved me all the time, that is the proof, not some theory like a college professor teaches you. Interesting how this all works.

As a parent, you must grow up. Who cares what society has portrayed since the sexual revolution of the '60s, on television, or in social media? Have we forgotten who we are? Have we forgotten to become parents? To be a full adult, you must be the maturity, grace, and self-discipline. It's your job as a parent. You are not their friend; you are their parent. It's up to you to hand off those traits to your kids, so they become fully formed, fully grown women and men. Coddling them and making excuses for them will only lead to many problems in the future. You must show them how to dress right, to dress appropriately by setting the example. As parents, we must set the template for what is admirable. Should we not, what will your children become?

The only way the world and society are ever going to change is to change children's minds by teaching them manners, respect, love, forgiveness, tolerance, and love of their country. That could be a whole other book. To get them educated and off their smartphones, video games, and movies. Away from the violence and sex that permeates our society. Teach them to live their life according to the higher power's blueprint. Not be racists or judgmental or to live by certain religious, social, or political ideologies. Live within the laws of the country they reside and by the universal law of treating others how they would like to be treated. Stand for what they believe in and not waiver-to live in a world of love inside their minds, hearts, souls, and the real world. Live fruitful lives of caring for others while loving themselves. Live righteously by doing the right thing all the time no matter how painful and lonely they may become. Not wander off their path and to have as much fun along the way. Love their life no matter the hardships that they will face. You must teach them these things, yes, you!

Love works in many ways, and being a parent is probably the hardest job you will ever have. It takes a bunch of responsibility and time. You are now in charge of a little creature, your creature. Nothing is worse than a bad kid or dog; we have all been there. Make your child the sweetest, fairest, smartest, and most loving you can. You must be the one that shows them this. Give them a chance. Break the cycle should you have had a tough childhood with distracted parents. Let go of any of your selfishness and use love when solving all the issues. Teach lessons and be real.

Read to them and discipline them. Teach about nature and the universe's unconditional love. Make them ten times better than you could ever be. That is how they will repay you when you get old. With respect and caring, you taught them. They will become your parent one day. Teach them the right way to become a thoughtful, respectful human being, and you will sleep fine. It will be one less thing to fear in life and something to look forward to while spending some of your last days on earth with the child you built into an adult. Someone you love and who loves you. What a beautiful concept. Be a great parent!

Learning to Say No

"Half of the troubles of this life can be traced to saying yes too quickly and not saying no soon enough"
– Josh Billings

You know, the older I get, the less I know. Like saying no. Some studies claim by saying no that we can add ten years to our life. Wow. I rarely said no my entire life. Not until I started reflecting on myself and analyzing my actions over the years did I understand the power of no. It would have saved me from many unpleasant experiences. Some of us look upon life as just this thing and never step back and understand why we are here, at least most of us do. What some of us do not realize is that this is a fraction of time in history (time doesn't exist, it's human-made), and some of us waste it doing things we just do not want to do. I am not saying do whatever the hell you want as there are things like being educated, being healthy, taking care of your family and children. Learning to love and so on that we must do, no matter how we feel about them. So why do we put ourselves in situations we do not like? What does saying no do for us?

My manager invited me over to his house for a party that he throws every year. One year he invited me, about two weeks before, and asked again at work the Monday before whether I would attend. I said you bet, buddy. Fast forward a couple of days, and he was out of the office. He is never out; the guy is very dedicated and one of the most beautiful souls I have ever met. I check in on him, and he tells me that his daughter has the flu. His daughter lives at home with him, the place where the party will be. That year the flu hit the US hard with thirty-two people dying in the county I lived in alone.

I had been ill a few weeks before; I mentioned the story earlier. I thought I am always thinking, sometimes a curse, and most times, this brings clarity to a situation. The day came for the party, and he said that she broke her fever. However, the flu is all I thought about, not the party, not the food, not the drinks, not the conversations, not the band, nothing but the flu. I had to tell him no, I am not coming. I felt his sadness as we have a bond. I felt a little bad at first; however, I have learned to let decisions I make go and not living in the past with guilt. What I am saying is that by saying no, I felt better. I felt relieved that I was not going. The worry, the fear, was now all gone. I just did not want to expose myself to illness. Something inside me said to say no, and I went with it. That was my soul guiding me. Listen when that voice tells you something. Everything worked out fine; after all, I just missed a party.

We all have a busy life filled with perceived distractions. We have friends and perceived friends of all kinds at work, where we live, places we go, etc.... One day, this guy, an old friend, asked me to help him move an aquarium. I said sure, buddy, no problem. He said next weekend. That morning, I was busy working out and went for a long run. I had set up my birthday party at the pool that day with a caterer, and it was to begin around one-thirtyish. I never give a specific time for things at the pool that would be a colossal mistake and filled with expectations. He texts me, and I called him, it was about ten-thirty AM. He said, "when are you coming over? I have the aquarium, an entertainment system, a washer, and a dryer and a few other things."

I said hey, "didn't you say it was just an aquarium?" I told him no that I had this party I was hosting and didn't have the time for all of that, just the aquarium. He flew off the handles. I could have helped him the next day as he was just moving from one apartment building to another across the street. Six months later, I saw this guy out at a local bar, and he gazed at me for a while from across the room. I told him "hi" when I walked by to put some music on the electronic jukebox. He waved me over on the way back and said, "all I needed is for you is to say sorry." I took a deep breath, took the high road, and remembered that love conquers all. I told him, "I'm sorry." And that was it, no more thought about it. That is why connecting to a higher power and understanding that forgiveness and peace is the height of unconditional love. These stories are as many situations in life we find ourselves. By saying no to specific circumstances, you relieve yourself of going through the motions and make yourself happier. Saying no is tough for some people; however, in the end, it just may add some peace to your life.

I was at dinner one evening with my buddy, and he was having relationship issues. We discussed the many problems, and I just told him relationships are supposed to build each other up and grow. When they do nothing but destroy you and your energy, it's time for an exit strategy. He said, what do I do to get her off my mind? I asked him, what has that voice inside you been telling you your whole life? What do you want to accomplish? He said a few things and then began down a road discussing how he only focused on his child, which is an excellent thing for a parent. I then turned the conversation back to what he wanted to accomplish in life. He had no idea. I said make a list of what you want to achieve and whenever you are having dark thoughts of the relationship or life, turn to the list and put these ideas into the universe. Focus your energy on those ideas. Whatever you say about yourself and put into the world is what you will become. Make them become a reality. He then said in his whole life he never said no, he always sacrificed his life for his loved ones no matter what. He never had time for himself to accomplish his dreams. I told him you have to say no to grow. We all must focus our energy on ourselves and make ourselves happy before we make others happy. Saying no to certain situations opens your path of life for your dreams. Say no when you know it's right, say yes when it's appropriate.

Saying yes is so much easier than saying no. We all like things to be Zen and tranquil. However, when we always say yes to people, when do we have the time for us? We can only do so much in a day. When we sit back and think and say no first, we open time for ourselves in the right situations. We have time for us to do something we enjoy. When we continue to say yes, we do not have the time for our happiness. I am not saying be selfish here; I am saying we all need time for ourselves, to build on our own life. To work on the things to build up our minds, bodies, and soul. To make ourselves better, channel our energy to our life and our destiny.

Should you always say yes, then you will drive yourself crazy? Your mind will still be spinning about that next event you scheduled. Say no to things. Relax. You are not conscious of your life. The whole point is to say yes to the things that make you happy. Say no to things that do not, that again does not mean not spending time with the person or people you love doing something they enjoy. You must learn to like things you never thought you would in this case. By saying no, you create space in your life to do something you deem necessary, you have time to work on your life's path and have the time to spend with the people you love. Say yes when it's right, say no when it doesn't. Sounds simple; however, this will open your life calendar, change your outlook on life, and help build your future.

REST

"Rest when you're weary. Refresh and renew yourself, your body, your mind, your spirit. Then get back to work."
– Ralph Martson

Do you get enough sleep? How much is enough? Is there a direct correlation between sleep, your mind, and your soul? Do your dreams make you aware of your future? Is rest designed to expand your soul's awareness? Sleep is a condition of body and mind. It typically occurs for several hours every night, in which the nervous system is relatively inactive, the eyes closed, the postural muscles relaxed, and consciousness is practically suspended. On a spiritual level, sleep is defined as the soul leaving the body, expanding one's awareness, traveling through the cosmos, and demonstrating a vivid outlook on one's life. Let's discuss some aspects of sleep, so you understand it's not just going to bed and closing your eyes.

I have always been a big sleeper. Only in my older years when thinking about others or some issue that has not been the case. Your overall mental, physical, and spiritual health depend on sleep. Many diseases such as heart disease, diabetes, stroke, Alzheimer's, you name it, are on the list when you do not get enough sleep. Sleep also helps to relieve stress, which is affecting a vast swath of every society. We all need rest to maintain our health. Besides your physical health, your mental and spiritual health are the most valuable things you own. By resting correctly, you have the energy to live life to the fullest and make your dreams come true.

Sleeping is a long, unconscious mediation. You are giving your brain rest, and, in the meantime, your body rebuilds. Your soul needs this time for itself to expand its awareness. It takes a lot of energy to remain awake, so the universe's created sleep for your soul to live free and the ability to do anything without fear. Sleep allows your soul to cruise the universe for answers, through dreams, to anything that plagues your mind. When you pay attention to that aspect of sleep, you can answer the questions you have about yourself. Many dreams will lead you to the inner self and bring many benefits in your conscious, woken life.

Dreaming aside, the act of recognizing sleep as a therapeutic process of body and mind, as a reprieve from the physical plane, as a shift in consciousness, can all bolster your spiritual practice. Any act can be made sacred with intent and devotion. Sleep can answer questions and heal you. However, the more you churn, feel frustrated or depressed, the less rest you get. You awake tired and drained. And sometimes, we want to escape reality and sleep more. That is why it is essential to become balanced in life. It allows you to function and sleep on a deeper level to restore your batteries.

Sleep is natural and a physiological requisite to being awake and alive. Should one, through spiritual development, tap into the vast stores of cosmic energies, one can see the outcome of their dreams. Like any other activity, sleep can bring much spiritual benefit should one focus and apply themselves to those ends. Nearly every religion attribute at least a fraction of its basis to dreams. Because it's such a departure from the normal mode of conscious thought and we are still able to accommodate consciousness, great experiences are possible. When focused, lifelong questions and revelations can be received, otherworldly entities contacted, and much more. Many discoveries that plagued the human mind, the theory of relativity, electricity, and the manifest destiny of the United States occurred in dreams. See what Einstein, Tesla, and Washington did with those dreams? All things in the universe have the chance to happen every night. Not that every dream is necessarily spiritual, they are, without a doubt, one of the most universally accessible ways to experience the abundance of the universe. Dreams shine a light on what's going on inside of you.

Taking the time to get a good night's rest without all the distractions we face today adds to your ability to function normally in our chaotic world. You have the energy to accomplish whatever you are manifesting. When you achieve your goals, you feel better about yourself. That raises your vibration and attracts more accomplishment. And when we accomplish more things in life, we lift ourselves to a higher level that connects us with the universe. We manifest the thoughts and dreams we put into it. It's all connected. Get some rest and pay attention to your dreams!!!

Deadly Sins of Life

"Beware of monotony; it's the mother of all the deadly sins."
– Edith Wharton

So, you are getting religious on us? Believing in a higher power and believing in yourself takes faith. Faith is the belief in something that you cannot see or touch; however, you think it exists. Like love, your actions and words will show faith. It is the motives behind your words and actions that matter. What you speak out into the world is what you will become. Talk of good things and your dreams, not the negative stuff. Do unto others as you want to be done unto you. That is why faith in yourself, your words, and your thoughts are so important. Live your life with the values you believe are ethical, positive, and full of love. Refraining from the deadly sins in your thoughts, words, and actions will bring you salvation and closer to your inner self. You will shield yourself from all the drama in the world. And in time, bring out the love in others.

Faith and love in a higher power are not only showing up to some building to worship or give money; however, money does help the community. The message is merely a blueprint on how to live your life. Period. Instead of looking for a message every Sunday in a pew should you attend any religious service, be the message, and spread that love after you leave everywhere you go. Do not let humankind drive you away by their interpretation of what "they believe." Believe what you think brings you closer to your dreams, the higher power, and the love that fills your heart. Find that love and connect with it.

Below are the deadly sins and how to overcome them. Should you stay away from these motives and follow these basic guidelines of life, you will build your inner vibration. People will know that you are a person who cares not only for themselves; however, they believe in helping and changing the lives of others around them for good.

Envy = the desire to have an item or experience that someone else possesses

Gluttony = excessive ongoing consumption of food or drink

Greed = an excessive pursuit of material possessions

Lust = an uncontrollable passion or longing, especially for sexual desires

Pride = excessive view of one's self without regard to others.

Sloth = excessive laziness or the failure to act and utilize one's talents

Wrath = uncontrollable emotions of anger and hate towards another person

Curing the Deadly Sins of Life

Kindness = cures envy by placing the desire to help others above the need to supersede them

Temperance = cures gluttony by implanting the desire to be healthy, therefore making one fit to serve others

Charity or love = heals greed by putting the desire to help others above storing up treasure for one's self

Chastity or Self-control = cures lust by controlling passion and leveraging that energy for the good of others

Humility = cures pride by removing one's ego and boastfulness, therefore allowing the attitude of service

Diligence or Zeal = cures slothfulness by placing the best interest of others above the life of ease and relaxation.

Patience = cures wrath by taking time to understand others' needs and desires before acting or speaking.

What the universe does not like for us to do to others: A proud look, a lying tongue, hands that shed innocent blood, a heart that devises wicked plans, feet that are swift in running to evil, a false witness who speaks lies, and one who sows discord among brethren.

Deeds of the flesh are immorality, impurity, sensuality, idolatry, sorcery, enmities, strife, jealousy, outbursts of anger, disputes, dissensions, factions, envying, carousing.

Master the curing qualities, and you master what we are all here on this planet to do, love one another.

Exercise your Mind, Body and Soul

"The mind is the key; the heart is the door; the soul is corridor; the universe is the destination."
– Anonymous

I know this is part of the title, and you are probably looking for this to be a big section. That is not the case. Never assume anything. Seek the knowledge. Throughout the book is where you will find this information. Let's look at some basic things to do every day of your life that allow you to grow internally, get healthier, and what you seek in life through your mind, body, and soul.

Exercise your Mind

Life is full of fascinating things. Beautiful things, smelly things, ugly things, evil things, you name it. There is a lot out there. Why not learn about them all? Learn as much as you can about everything; history, religion, math, science, languages, food, coffee, people, I think you get it. Instead of worrying about others and yourself every day, pray instead. Gain the knowledge to take care of them and yourself. Read, go to school, and graduate. Keep graduating from everything in life. Seek the expertise to fulfill your life, learn it. We all have something in us that fears, overcome the fear, and be successful. Learn the true meaning of your life. Let go to grow and rest to be blessed. Stay away from the thoughts that hold you back. Train your mind always to think the glass is half full, not half empty. The knowledge to do whatever in your life is in you, tap in!

Exercise your Body

Well, here we are in one of my favorite sections. Remember, I used to lay around, eat terribly, and consume alcohol frequently? I allowed my ego and past to run my life. However, found that happiness was inside me the whole time. I am unable now to get enough exercise. How did I change that? Should you want to change your body and get healthy, it's not some magic food or pill; it's you! Start slowly by walking or riding a bike, stationary should you have access to one, and work your way up. Get off fast food! The fundamentals of losing weight are burning more calories than you consume. Go to the grocery store and start eating more salads, not with creamy fat-filled dressings, eat more fish, limit your red meat, and keep the carbs minimum. Your diet should only consist of 10% meat. Stay off sodas, sugar, and salt. High blood sugar levels are associated with memory decline. High sodium in the blood raises your blood pressure that increases the risk of stroke. Stay away from processed foods.

Once you begin this, start exercising three days a week. Join a gym or lookup exercise videos and do them at home. Work on your core. Start lifting light, even you ladies, and work your way up. Hire a trainer. You will be sore. Working out and running or walking alleviates stress and allows you to sleep better. Do not eat late. Get rest every night. Stay away from anything, causing you stress. You are what you eat. Clear your mind and do not fear what others think of you. Keep pushing yourself. Practice new exercises. Recover. Work your way up to five or six days of training. Park farther out in a parking lot, so you walk more and don't get your vehicle all dinged up. There are many things you can do to change your life. Getting in shape is one of them.

Exercise your Soul

Your soul is the very core of your being. It's the energy inside you that keeps your heart ticking. It's thousands of dust particles formed in the outer reaches of space that have come together to make you. No one on earth is exactly like you. Embrace the beauty of that. The universe has given you this beautiful soul for you to show yourself the love of life. Share that with the world and the people you love and that love you. Let your abilities shine; do not be fearful of being looked upon differently or being successful. Thank yourself every morning for being you. Practice meditation. Be thoughtful and generous with your time and money. Take in nature and all her glory. Think about how beautiful just being alive is. Get out in the woods to view nature and ponder your thoughts. Pay attention. Live in the present and do what makes you happy. Your heart is the gateway to your soul. Love is the gateway to solving all of life's mysteries. Be in tune with the vibration of your soul. It will guide you to your salvation.

THE PHOENIX

"Now, this is not the end. It is not even the beginning of the end. But it is, perhaps, the end of the beginning."
– Winston Churchill

In Greek Mythology, the phoenix is a long-lived bird that cyclically regenerates or is born again. The phoenix rises from the ashes of its predecessor. Your past negative thoughts are your ashes, your future is the reborn phoenix, and your present is flying joyfully high above the clouds. Live in the clouds with high thoughts about your life and yourself and in the season of rebirth. Why not? One of my friends responds to everything with "Why not." What a sense of living without fearing anything. Just like you can!

Here you are at the end of the book. Your journey had begun long before you read this; however, you are probably looking at the path very differently now. Everything in life ends, relationships, businesses, loves, and life itself; however, that's when there is a new beginning. Every ending is the beginning of some beginnings end-you are at the new beginning, not the end. Death is just a new beginning, quit fearing it. What you seek is not behind you; it's ahead of you.

Life is something many of us will never understand and will never take the time to dive into ourselves to figure out. However, we all want to live a happy life and just do not know how to go about it. Life's journey is to learn love for oneself and heal all the emotional pain on the inside. Life is an inside job to heal your wounds, find people that love you and your purpose. We are all on this journey. The understanding you are on a quest to figure out your purpose is when you pay attention to your life, dreams, and relationships. Life is precious and about finding peace and love while using love to solve all internal and external issues. Living life through the eyes of others and searching for their approval; brings emotional turmoil and drama to our lives. In the end, all pain is self-induced. Sad when you realize how much time and energy you have wasted. Only you make yourself suffer. Self-love and self-forgiveness are the paths to begin the journey. It's the understanding you are a spirit having a human experience, and you are on a quest. A quest to find self-love, love for others, love for all living things, and to understand you are loved by the universe unconditionally.

We will all have a karmic event in our lives that forces us to face our inner selves. When the event occurs, be aware and pay attention to your inner voice as your soul is guiding you to figure out the lessons that plague your mind and keep you distracted. The tests are all the hardships, betrayals, and loss of loved ones. By recognizing your ego when it rears its ugly head, you let go of all the external drama, attachments, and people who cause you inner pain. You then allow yourself to learn the lessons of forgiveness of others, self-forgiveness, love, love of self, love of others, and unconditional love. You end the ego madness. Then your perception of self and others changes, and you find the joy and happiness in life by allowing yourself to be the eagle that flies above the drama and storms. You recognize what is essential in your life and your value, your real value, your soul. You come to this understanding by finding the biggest love of your life, yourself. You understand only you complete you. You make you happy by listening to your soul. What can you take with you when you die besides your soul?

Everything ends. Everything in the universe will end. The earth will end. Our lives will end. However, throughout our experience, we must learn to loosen the perceived control of every decision's end. When we struggle along this path for power, some type of control, we lose control. Then we either want to control everything or think as though we have no control. We must learn endings and letting go of the perceived control is what brings growth to our lives. It brings growth to our mind, body, and soul. We must instead seek to control our thoughts and emotions as we all believe the world should change in some way; we instead need only to change ourselves. That is a new beginning to within to become the higher self we all have inside of us and end the ego's drama of control.

Your thoughts are what creates your life; it's the mirror. By believing your ideas and dreams, you can live any life you choose. Living in the negativity of the past will only destroy you and your relationships. Living in the positivity of the present will present opportunities to grow your life. Manifest your life, put the images into the universe, believe, speak it, and believe in yourself. Stop and look around at the beauty of the world instead of complaining. It's a fantastic planet. Find something to be thankful for instead of hanging onto something negative. Every test is a learning experience, and every test, should you pass, is a lesson. Take the positive out of every experience, surrender the negatives. Be the giver, not the taker. Be thankful you wake up every morning and live life with a smile on your face. Then do and say things from the heart. Live life every day as though you are on vacation. Channel the love of the universe through you. Love and happiness come from within, not the external, and share it with others. That will attract what you seek.

Life is about love, people, and the love of people, not worldly things. Once you practice this, your whole life will change, and you will attract the people and experiences to unfold and guide you to your life purpose. Life is full of wonders, thoughts, and experiences, get out there, and enjoy them. Attempt not to miss them with destructive thoughts about others and yourself. Spend your time with the people that lift you and love you, not the ones that bring you down. Understand your subconscious mind and correct the evil thoughts. Feel your energy and recognize the power, every thought, every word, and every action. Stay on your path by loving and finding yourself. Pay attention and live in the present. Away from wicked thoughts of the past, and the fearful thoughts about the future. Let them go and use your universe connected mind to guide you. Stay in the present, and you will attract what you seek. Have some fun and live every day like it's your last on this planet. Keep growing and get out of your comfort zone daily.

Growing every day consists of many different thoughts about self and others. A process of learning to understand the self, people's actions, and why we tick the way they do. To understand and connect to the universe and its love. To show that universal love for others. To not judge, to forgive, especially ourselves. To understand good and evil live within ourselves, not only in the external world. To be open to criticism, constructive that is, and to be a great mirror that changes someone's life for the good. To be yourself all the time, your true self. To use the force of love and convey that message as it always dwells inside you. To be a leader and be thankful for what you have, not upset about what you do not have. To give thanks to the universe and your parents no matter the struggle as they both got you here. To understand all the events since the beginning of time for you even to be alive. To hold hands and love one another. To put your smartphone down and enjoy the world. To keep loving no matter what, even your perceived enemies. There will be relationship failures, and issues are opportunities to fix something; they are just growing mechanisms. To fix yourself by respecting yourself and setting boundaries with people.

Be a good partner, father, mother, and spouse. To understand your love's childhood and the struggles they may have faced so you can help, not feed the hurt. To know there is someone out there for everyone, they already exist, stay on your path, and find them. To be a great friend who helps, forgives and loves. To stay away from becoming a drug addict or an alcoholic. To quit wasting opportunities to enjoy life with thoughts of guilt, shame, or fear. To stop beating yourself up for everything. To live in the present with a smile and to be happy on the inside.

Should I not find an end to this chapter, it will never end; however, that is a new beginning. Just like every relationship, you will ever have in life will end, whether good, bad, or death, it will end. The only relationship that will not end is the one you have with yourself. Be your best friend, not your worst enemy. Cherish the time, build memories with the people you love, and be present to enjoy the time. Find inner happiness by releasing the control of being right all the time. Set your mind right every day by setting aside some quiet time unplugging from the digital world. Take into consideration the emotions of others. Understand inner peace is the answer to your salvation, dreams, and ultimate happiness. Wake up every day and use your energy to fulfill your life purpose, not wasted on bad relationships and people who do not care about you and your family. Understand sometimes the higher power's greatest gifts bestowed upon you are unanswered prayers, and his greatest blessings are the hurtful actions and words from others. Those are all lessons to within.

The universe is demonstrating your future to you by putting you in the fire, do not hang on to hurtful events in your life, letting them go, and the bounds will disappear. Stay firm on removing your ego and help others remove theirs. Greatness begins in your heart, not from the accolades you receive from others. The recognition comes when you believe in yourself and unselfishly accomplish your dreams through helping others. The journey is about love, forgiveness, and happiness, tend your garden, and remove the rocks and weeds. You are the only one who can look inside and do this. It's the six-and-a-half inches between your ears is the toughest part of life. You are a seed, surround yourself with fertile soil, and grow tall.

Happiness lives in your mind, heart, and soul, and you are the one that must put it there. Conquer yourself, and you will conquer the changing world. Use love to solve all the issues you face in life. Be a kid at heart, not tainted and judgmental. View the real reality, not the one where you think it should be this way or that way, and stay away from the anger caused by this. Stay true to your values. Let go of all the rage and fear caused by others. Live in reality, not some made-up thing in your mind, view it through your eyes, and feel it in your heart. Do not judge people; do your best to show them, love. Not everyone thinks like you, understand that. Get some rest and get out there and exercise your body. Practice the four L's of life every day, Living, Loving, Learning, and Laughing. Stop discounting yourself. Stay away from the deadly sins and listen to your intuition and the little voice inside you. Follow that voice, understand to say no sometimes, realize you are on a journey to find your purpose in life.

Understand the hardships and recognize the karmic events. Those events lead you to self-love and your value. How people treat you is their karma; how you respond is yours. There is only one way to bring you joy and happiness in this lifetime, understand and connect to your vibration. Do not allow the external world to drive your life, surrender to the all connected universe, and abundance. The journey of life is to go within to find the unconditional love for yourself. Manifest your dreams and believe in them. Rewire your mind to be happy to share your love and happiness with the ones that love you. Tell people you love them, that's where it's at in life. And always be exercising your Mind, Body, and Soul. Get over your drama already. Love is the answer to everything. Everybody deserves to be loved, especially loved by themselves. I believe in you, and I love you!!!

The Journey Continues

Through writing this book and the journey itself, I failed many tests with my ego, thoughts, and lack of paying attention. However, I recognized some of them and working to correct them. Remember to take the advice you give to others. Life is full of lessons, and until you learn them, they will continue to plague you until you pass away. Learn them now so you can enjoy your life. When you let go of your ego, you become happy, free, and let go of foolish thoughts that cloud your destiny and happiness. I still must deal with society; however, I am society just like I am traffic, and so are you, so stop getting so upset on the road. Surrender the ego and enjoy the peace. The paragraphs below are a few examples of where the journey has taken me.

Think about these questions as you continue your journey: Do you understand now that you are on a journey? You are a spirit? You can manifest anything? You love yourself? The only relationship that lasts your entire life is the one you have with yourself. You need to release the past? Everything that happened in your life occurs just how it was supposed to for you to be the person you are today. You are the eagle that flies above the storms and drama? Your vibration is what is attracts your dreams? You seek to cleanse your mind, body, and soul of the darkness and replace it with the light of love? You are here for a reason? You have a purpose?

As I stated, my journey began long ago when I was five; however, I realized the journey started again, and this book is just the tip of the iceberg. By practicing the many topics, I wrote about, I have experienced so many incredible things. I used to get up and go to work, or to the gym or the pool or the ranch or the coast, okay you get it and just go. Now I know everywhere I go is an excellent adventure. I have met so many incredible people and changed their perspective on life, and they have changed mine. It's not strange to me anymore that a perfect stranger comes up to me, we start talking, and they tell me their whole life story; it just happens. Also, that so many spiritual people have helped me. Mind-blowing sometimes. However, that is the path. Change who you are on the inside will change your whole life on the outside. This world is an inside game, recognize it. Like so many things in life, people live in a world that they dream of in their heads.

My past real life was sitting around and thinking about old girlfriends and old friends and wondering what happened or about some stupid thing I did when I was younger. Probably like a bunch of people. Then hey, someone who I perceived as a friend, would call or send a text to come to a bar or party or somewhere. Yeah!!! Then go to a bar and get plastered with a fake friend who was there drinking away the same drama. Should this be you, I hope you understand you are wasting your life; you are missing the boat. Life is about being happy, sharing love, taking care of people, changing people's lives for the better, and living it up. Life is about love and people and building lasting memories forever, not some drunken party. Get over it.

One of my "living like I'm on vacation" things is playing water volleyball for the last twenty years. I still do, I alluded to that earlier. The pool is full of people that I never thought would come together the way we have. The guys out there would show up, argue almost every play, and want to fight; it was mayhem. I stepped into the league ten years ago was still a foolish man and went along with it. However, three years ago, my journey started creeping into all my thoughts everywhere. I got in shape, hung out, set up the pool area, and starting using love with positive reflections on and off the court. I raised the net eight inches as people were getting fingers and thumbs broken. Initiated Rule #1, which is to have fun no matter what you are doing. Brought plenty of beer, shots, and food and helped enact a no touching the net rule; real volleyball rules. After two years, the whole place changed, everyone, just about everyone did, and now that place is full of fun, excitement, and love. People come down to the pool to just watch us play while they hang with their spouses, children, or friends. People come by just to say hi. People bring us four hundred jello shots and set up a catered party with shrimp, chicken, and beef fajitas. People leave and give us all their beer. I could keep going. One example of how the journey changed me, however, also changed the whole area and the people around me at the pool. You can do the same thing; it's in you. Love is in you.

Through the journey, I had no idea sometimes why things were happening. I started traveling and doing things outside my comfort zone and began meeting people, strangers. One trip I took to the coast to visit and fish with my uncle. We would go out early in the morning, launch the boat, catch fish, load the boat back on the trailer, wash the boat, clean the fish, and eat lunch. He would then do his thing, and that left the whole afternoon to myself. I would go down to this place every day and have some drinks. They would grill my fresh fish, and I would work on the book. People would show up, and we would chat, and they would ask me what I was doing down there. I would tell them fishing with my uncle, screwing off, and writing a book. One day a lady came in on Wednesday, to be exact. She immediately responded with a vibration conversation and said that she had seen me earlier at the grocery store. Something called her to that place as she rarely went out. We hit it off and began discussing all kinds of things. I went over to her home that trip, and she gave me many ideas for the book and the next book. Somewhere I would have never imagined a small fishing community on the Texas Coast. It's everywhere be ready.

Another day I out having a few drinks with some guys from work. We went to this place by work after five PM. They all left around seven-fifteen, so something told me to go by this other place for a few beers. I stopped by and hung out for about thirty minutes. A young girl was there that I knew, and I said, "Hello, how are you?" She started crying immediately. I consoled her and told her that her value was not the guy's approval that left her over the conversation. She calmed down and said she would attempt to understand and let him go. She left with a half-smile. I only hope she understands that every hardship is a lesson to within. Some other people I knew were there, and I said "Hello", and they said "Sit down" at their table. The wife said she saw what I had done and thought it was very thoughtful.

I said it was my duty as something inside me said to do it. She said, "Your spirit?" I said yes, and off we went. We talked for over an hour, and they gave me a book. The husband went to his truck and brought it back. It was about a neurosurgeon's journey into the afterlife while he was in a coma, spiritual stuff. Fascinating stuff. As I have said, it's all around you. Find love, quit judging people, and hanging out with people for all the wrong reasons. Find your journey within, and your life's purpose will appear.

When I started traveling around, people and I would begin speaking and talking about all kinds of things, mostly on airplanes. Somehow, I always ended up next to an older woman, what great conversations. I would be working on this book, and they would ask what I was doing. I told them and what it was about, and they would ask whether they could read some. I said sure as I was unsure how this whole thing would go over. One story is that this lady read the book for five minutes and began to cry. I was nervous, I admit, she said, wow, my friends and I were just talking about this stuff. You are light years ahead of me on this. She kept reading off and on for an hour, and we would discuss it. At the end of the flight, she told me, "You just changed my life forever." I was semi-stunned. We exchanged numbers, and I still hear from her now and then. Almost the same story with another woman on an airplane back from

West Palm Beach, Florida. A year later, I met her for lunch in Austin, Texas, with her stepson to help him through a difficult time.

I affirm when you live by just a few simple rules, you will change other people's lives and your own. Rules are, use the love given to all of us from the higher power to solve all issues and treat people like you want to be treated. How people treat you is their karma; how you respond is yours. I used to follow; however, my following days are over, now I just follow through. Remember these few things, and you will be successful in your journey. These are only a few of about twenty or so crazy intense stories, some in the book, I experienced while writing this book. Remember to live the love vibration, use love, and get in touch with your soul; you can conquer anything.

SIDE NOTES

Dear Writer,
 dear friend. A person of ♡ joy + grace.
 A joy to know you our friend. Beauty in (appearance) + inside. Look to the next 2 yrs. Look, Look, to the Rainbo follow it + follow your dreams.

 Ruth
 mom

P.S. You have given Ruth + Jo <u>Xtra</u> time

About the Author

This is Terence Michael Shannon's first book. He was born in San Antonio, Texas, in the early seventies, has two older brothers, fifty-three first cousins and raised in a Catholic household. He played many sports, mainly football, baseball, and basketball, ran a small amount of track, and won several city championships on his swim team growing up. His father's family hailed from Downers Grove, Chicago, Illinois, and his mother's family settled a little town, Castroville, Texas. Both parents were born in San Antonio, Texas, and married in 1963. He believes he is half German, a quarter Irish and a quarter Norwegian. He played quarterback in middle school, receiver and punter in high school and pitched throughout his childhood to a college scholarship. He has one son who won a Texas State Championship in both high school football and rugby.

Note from the Author

Word-of-mouth is crucial for any author to succeed. If you enjoyed *Get Over Your Drama Already*, please leave a review online—anywhere you are able. Even if it's just a sentence or two. It would make all the difference and would be very much appreciated.

Thanks!
Terence

Thank you so much for reading one of our

Motivational & Inspirational books.

If you enjoyed our book, please check out our recommendation for your next great read!

This Side Up by Amy Mangan

"*This Side Up* will leave you feeling relieved, not alone, hopeful, and grateful for a friend and writer like Amy Mangan who inspires us to reframe our let downs, have some laughs, and embrace life with all of its beautiful unexpected messes."

–Stacy Strazis, former producer *The Oprah Winfrey Show* and *CNN*

View other Black Rose Writing titles at www.blackrosewriting.com/books and use promo code **PRINT** to receive a **20% discount** when purchasing.

www.ingramcontent.com/pod-product-compliance
Lightning Source LLC
Chambersburg PA
CBHW052026070526
44584CB00016B/1916